Getting Started with Pester 5

A Beginner's Guide

Owen Heaume

Apress®

Getting Started with Pester 5: A Beginner's Guide

Owen Heaume
West Sussex, UK

ISBN-13 (pbk): 979-8-8688-0305-5

ISBN-13 (electronic): 979-8-8688-0306-2

https://doi.org/10.1007/979-8-8688-0306-2

Managing Director, Apress Media LLC: Welmoed Spahr
Acquisitions Editor: Smriti Srivastava
Development Editor: Laura Berendson
Editorial Assistant: Kripa Joseph

Cover designed by eStudioCalamar
Cover image designed by Cover image from Pixabay

Distributed to the book trade worldwide by Springer Science+Business Media New York, 1 New York Plaza, Suite 4600, New York, NY 10004-1562, USA. Phone 1-800-SPRINGER, fax (201) 348-4505, e-mail orders-ny@springer-sbm.com, or visit www.springeronline.com. Apress Media, LLC is a California LLC and the sole member (owner) is Springer Science + Business Media Finance Inc (SSBM Finance Inc). SSBM Finance Inc is a **Delaware** corporation.

For information on translations, please e-mail booktranslations@springernature.com; for reprint, paperback, or audio rights, please e-mail bookpermissions@springernature.com.

Apress titles may be purchased in bulk for academic, corporate, or promotional use. eBook versions and licenses are also available for most titles. For more information, reference our Print and eBook Bulk Sales web page at http://www.apress.com/bulk-sales.

Any source code or other supplementary material referenced by the author in this book is available to readers on GitHub. For more detailed information, please visit https://www.apress.com/gp/services/source-code.

If disposing of this product, please recycle the paper

Table of Contents

About the Author

 **Owen Heaume** is a seasoned PowerShell programmer with a passion for crafting efficient solutions in the dynamic landscapes of Intune and Azure. Having recently embarked on a professional journey in PowerShell programming for a prominent company within their automation team, Owen is dedicated to mastering the intricacies of Pester, Azure DevOps, and adhering to best practices.

Owen has published books on deploying applications in Intune using PowerShell, deploying applications in ConfigMgr using PowerShell, and deploying language and regional settings using ConfigMgr. In this book, Owen shares insights gained from real-world experiences, providing readers with practical knowledge and a glimpse into the mind of a multifaceted professional thriving in the realms of technology.

About the Technical Reviewer

Kasam Shaikh is a prominent figure in India's artificial intelligence (AI) landscape, holding the distinction of being one of the country's first four Microsoft Most Valuable Professionals (MVPs) in AI. Currently he serves as a senior architect. Kasam boasts an impressive track record as an author, having authored five best-selling books dedicated to Azure and AI technologies. Beyond his writing endeavors, Kasam is recognized as a Microsoft Certified Trainer (MCT) and an influential tech YouTuber (@mekasamshaikh). He also leads the largest online Azure AI community, known as DearAzure | Azure INDIA, and is a globally renowned AI speaker. His commitment to knowledge sharing extends to contributions to Microsoft Learn, where he plays a pivotal role.

Within the realm of AI, Kasam is a respected subject matter expert (SME) in generative AI for the cloud, complementing his role as a senior cloud architect. He actively promotes the adoption of No Code and Azure OpenAI solutions and possesses a strong foundation in Hybrid and Cross-Cloud practices. Kasam Shaikh's versatility and expertise make him an invaluable asset in the rapidly evolving landscape of technology, contributing significantly to the advancement of Azure and AI.

In summary, Kasam Shaikh is a multifaceted professional who excels in both technical expertise and knowledge dissemination. His contributions span writing, training, community leadership, public speaking, and architecture, establishing him as a true luminary in the world of Azure and AI. Kasam was recently awarded as top voice in AI by LinkedIn, making him the sole exclusive Indian professional acknowledged by both Microsoft and LinkedIn for his contributions to the world of artificial intelligence!

CHAPTER 1

Unveiling the Power of Pester

Welcome to the exciting world of Pester! In this chapter, we will embark on a journey to demystify the art of testing in PowerShell using the powerful tool called Pester. If you are new to PowerShell or testing frameworks, fear not; this guide is designed especially for you. Pester is not just any testing framework – it's your key to ensuring your PowerShell scripts are robust, reliable, and perform exactly as you intend.

In the upcoming sections, we will unravel the fundamentals of Pester. We'll begin by understanding what Pester is and why it holds a crucial place in the toolkit of every PowerShell developer. You'll learn about the compelling reasons to incorporate Pester into your scripting workflow, empowering you to write code with confidence.

We'll guide you through the installation process, ensuring you have the latest version of Pester ready to use.

But our exploration doesn't conclude there. In this chapter, we'll introduce you to the diverse spectrum of testing: unit tests, acceptance tests, and integration tests. These tests, much like different roles in a theatrical script, serve distinct purposes. Just as a director carefully selects actors for different scenes, you'll learn to choose the right test type for various scenarios in your coding journey. Whether you're validating individual components, interacting with real systems, or staging integrated functions, you'll have the tools to script tests that match your specific needs.

O. Heaume, *Getting Started with Pester 5*, https://doi.org/10.1007/979-8-8688-0306-2_1

We'll then navigate the intricate landscape of Pester files and their structure. By understanding the anatomy of these files, you'll lay a sturdy foundation for crafting well-organized and potent tests.

Whether you're a novice stepping into the PowerShell realm or a seasoned developer eager to refine your testing expertise, this chapter promises to furnish you with vital insights to kickstart your Pester journey.

What Is Pester?

Pester, in the realm of PowerShell, is not just a testing framework; it's a game-changer. Imagine having a reliable assistant by your side, carefully checking your PowerShell scripts for errors, ensuring they perform as expected, and providing you with the peace of mind that your code is robust. That assistant is Pester.

At its core, Pester is a testing framework specifically tailored for PowerShell. It's designed to simplify the process of writing and running tests for your PowerShell scripts and functions. But it's not just about spotting bugs; Pester encourages a mindset of proactive development. With Pester, you can validate your code's functionality, ensure it handles various scenarios, and confirm it responds correctly to different inputs.

Pester operates on a simple yet profound principle: **automated testing is your safety net**. It allows you to write tests that mimic real-world interactions with your scripts. By simulating different usage scenarios, input variations, and edge cases, you can be confident that your PowerShell code behaves as intended under diverse conditions.

Why Use Pester?

In the early days of my PowerShell journey, the notion of incorporating Pester into my workflow seemed like an unnecessary complication. I had already carefully crafted my scripts, ensuring they worked flawlessly on my system. The prospect of investing more time in writing additional code for testing felt daunting. I questioned, "Why add this layer of complexity when my scripts were already running smoothly?"

What I didn't realize then was that Pester isn't just about finding bugs or ensuring basic functionality. It's a powerful ally that elevates your scripts from functional to exceptional. Here's why taking that initial step to embrace Pester can transform your PowerShell experience:

1. **Automated assurance:** Pester acts as your automated quality control mechanism. It tirelessly validates your code, freeing you from the burden of manual testing. With Pester, you can be confident that your scripts are always in top-notch condition, no matter how many times you modify them.

2. **Confidence in code changes:** As your scripts evolve, ensuring they remain stable becomes vital. Pester empowers you to confidently refactor and enhance your code. By running a suite of tests, you can instantly identify if any recent changes have unintended consequences, enabling you to catch issues before they escalate.

3. **Effective collaboration:** Imagine sharing your scripts with team members or contributors. Pester ensures that your code behaves consistently across different environments. It becomes the common language that bridges the gap between developers, fostering collaboration and collective progress.

4. **Saves time in the long run:** Initially, writing tests might seem like an additional effort, but it's an investment that pays off over time. Detecting and fixing issues early prevents potential disasters down

the line. The time saved by avoiding manual bug hunting far outweighs the time spent crafting tests.

5. **Quality documentation:** Pester tests serve as living documentation for your code. They provide clear examples of how your functions and modules are meant to be used. This documentation becomes invaluable, especially when revisiting your own code after a considerable time gap or when onboarding new team members.

6. **Proactive problem solving:** Pester doesn't just find problems; it anticipates them. By simulating various scenarios and inputs, you can proactively identify potential weaknesses in your code. Addressing these vulnerabilities before they manifest in real-world usage enhances the resilience of your scripts.

In essence, Pester isn't merely about testing; it's about empowering your scripts to reach their full potential. The beauty of Pester lies in its seamless integration with PowerShell. If you're already familiar with PowerShell, learning Pester is a natural next step in enhancing your scripting arsenal. Embracing Pester equips you with the tools to create robust, reliable, and maintainable PowerShell solutions. So, take the plunge, invest a bit of time now, and watch your scripts shine in the long run. Pester isn't just a testing framework; it's your ticket to PowerShell excellence.

Installing Pester

Installing Pester is a straightforward process, ensuring you have a robust testing environment for your PowerShell scripts. Pester can be installed on any Windows computer with PowerShell version 3 or higher, although it's advisable to use PowerShell version 5 or 7 for the best experience.

Microsoft recognized the power of Pester and included it by default in Windows 10 and 11. However, the default versions might not always be the latest, and updating them can be tricky. Here's the recommended method to ensure you have the most up-to-date and easily maintainable version of Pester installed.

1. **Removing the Preinstalled Version:** If you're dealing with an older version of Pester, it's best to remove it completely. Run the following script shown in Listing 1-1 in an administrative PowerShell window.

Listing 1-1. Uninstalling legacy Pester

```
$module = "C:\Program Files↵
\WindowsPowerShell\Modules\Pester"
takeown /F $module /A /R
icacls $module /reset
icacls $module /grant "*S-1-5-32-544:F"↵
/inheritance:d /T
```

This script ensures the clean removal of the preinstalled Pester version, leaving your system ready for the latest installation.

2. **Installing the Latest Version:** With the old version removed, installing the latest Pester version is a breeze. Execute the following command in an administrative PowerShell window:

```
Install-Module Pester -Force
```

This command fetches and installs the latest version of Pester, ensuring you have the most advanced features at your fingertips.

3. **Easy Updates:** Managing updates is now hassle-free. To update Pester, simply run the following command in an administrative PowerShell window:

```
Update-Module Pester
```

This one-liner keeps your Pester framework current, incorporating any improvements or bug fixes seamlessly.

By following these steps, you ensure that Pester is not just installed on your system, but it's the latest, most potent version, and ready to empower your PowerShell testing endeavors. Now, let's dive into understanding Pester's file structure and its core components.

Navigating the Testing Landscape in PowerShell: Test Types

Welcome to the realm of testing in PowerShell, where scripts transform into robust and dependable solutions. Developers fine-tune their scripts through a series of carefully planned tests, much like orchestrating a captivating theater performance. Understanding the diverse landscape of testing methodologies is akin to exploring the varied techniques in the world of theater, each designed to bring out the best in a production.

In this section, we embark on a journey through the fundamental pillars of testing: unit tests, acceptance tests, and integration tests. Each test type is a unique lens through which developers can scrutinize their code, ensuring it not only meets its functional requirements but also weathers the challenges of real-world execution.

I'll employ a theater analogy (throughout this book) alongside conventional explanations to simplify the topic. Understanding these test types can be a bit overwhelming at first, so likening them to elements in a theater production might make the concepts more digestible.

Unit Tests

Unit tests focus on individual components or "units" of your code, typically functions or cmdlets. A unit test evaluates a specific piece of functionality in isolation. For example, if you have a function that converts lowercase text to uppercase, a unit test for this function would provide it with specific input and check if the output matches the expected result. The goal is to validate that the function performs as intended in various scenarios. Unit tests are isolated from the broader system and do not rely on external resources or dependencies.

The Analogy: Precision on Stage

Unit tests are the fundamental building blocks, akin to rehearsing scenes with precision in a theater production. Just as each actor and prop must be scrutinized for readiness and quality, unit tests meticulously examine individual components of your PowerShell script. These tests isolate functions, methods, or cmdlets, subjecting them to rigorous evaluations to ensure they perform their designated tasks flawlessly.

Integration Tests

Integration tests assess the interactions between different components or systems within your script. In the context of PowerShell, integration tests frequently involve connecting to external resources, databases, APIs, or other modules.

7

Unlike unit tests, integration tests focus on how these components collaborate and whether they work correctly when integrated. For example, if your script communicates with a database, an integration test would verify that the script can successfully connect, retrieve data, and handle responses. Mocking, where certain components are simulated to mimic real behavior, is often used in integration testing to isolate different parts of the system.

This book centers on both unit tests and integration tests, with a dedicated exploration of mocking for our integration tests, a topic that will be covered in a later chapter.

The Analogy: Orchestrating Script Performances

Integration tests resonate with the orchestration of diverse roles in a theater production. In a play, actors collaborate to bring characters to life, each contributing a unique essence to the overall performance. Similarly, integration tests explore how different components of your script interact. Whether it's connecting with databases, APIs, or external services, these tests ensure that the script functions seamlessly in a connected environment, much like the synergy required among actors for a compelling stage production.

Acceptance Tests

Acceptance tests evaluate the overall behavior of your script within the real system, simulating user interactions or system operations. Unlike unit tests, acceptance tests are less concerned with the internal logic of individual functions and more focused on the script's end-to-end functionality. These tests often deal with real-world scenarios, covering the entire application workflow. However, acceptance tests might not cover all edge cases, as their purpose is to validate general system behavior rather than specific conditions.

The Analogy: The Grand Stage Performance

Acceptance tests are the final act on stage, equivalent to presenting the complete play. Here, the entire script is performed, mirroring the way a theater production reaches the audience. These tests focus on the end-to-end functionality, mimicking real-world scenarios and user interactions. Just as the audience evaluates a play based on its presentation, engagement, and impact, acceptance tests gauge your script's performance, ensuring it satisfies user requirements and expectations.

Each type of test serves a specific purpose in ensuring the reliability of your PowerShell code. By employing a combination of unit tests to validate individual functions, acceptance tests to assess overall system behavior, and integration tests to test component interactions, you can create a robust testing strategy that thoroughly evaluates your scripts' functionality and performance.

As we delve into the intricacies of each test type, remember that testing is not merely a quality assurance task; it's a theatrical journey where developers refine their craft. So, prepare for a captivating exploration of PowerShell testing, where precision, completeness, and harmony are the guiding principles.

Pester Test Naming Convention and File Structure

In the world of Pester, naming conventions and file structures are your allies. Pester operates under the assumption that any file ending with *.tests.ps1* is a test file – a convention we highly recommend adhering to. While it's theoretically possible to alter this behavior, diving into such complexity is beyond the scope of this beginner's guide.

Why does Pester have this preference? Because Pester adores functions, and it challenges you to become a better coder by crafting functions that perform singular tasks. Writing functions this way not only aligns with PowerShell best practices but also makes your code highly testable. Consider a function like *Get-User*. It deserves its own file, aptly named *Get-User.ps1*. Correspondingly, your Pester test for this function should be named *Get-User.tests.ps1*. This clean separation ensures clarity in your project structure.

However, the naming standard can be further enhanced for differentiation. Adding a descriptor about the type of test being conducted is a common practice. For instance, if you're writing unit tests for *Get-User*, your test file could be named *Get-User.unit.tests.ps1*. Similarly, for integration tests, it could be *Get-User.integration.tests.ps1*, and for acceptance tests, *Get-User.acceptance.tests.ps1*.

This categorization not only clarifies the test type but also enables selective test execution – a topic we'll explore later in this book.

Keeping your .tests files in the same directory as the code they are testing is a wise choice. This organization fosters coherence and ensures that your tests are always in sync with your code. For example,

```
Get-User\
      Get-User.ps1
      Get-User.tests.ps1
```

If you're working with modules, a structured approach within module-related directories is advisable:

```
Get-User\
      Get-User\Public\
            Get-User.ps1
      Get-User\Tests\
            Get-User.tests.ps1
```

This modular arrangement facilitates a seamless workflow, making your tests as integral a part of your project as the code they validate. As you progress through this guide, you'll gain deeper insights into how such meticulous structuring can optimize your PowerShell projects.

Summary

In this introductory chapter, we delved into the fascinating world of Pester, the testing framework designed to empower PowerShell developers. We embarked on a journey to demystify testing in PowerShell, exploring the essential concepts that underpin Pester's functionality.

We began by understanding what Pester is and why it's indispensable for every PowerShell developer. Pester emerged as more than just a testing framework; it became the key to ensuring that PowerShell scripts are robust, reliable, and precisely execute their intended tasks. By embracing Pester, you unlock the potential to write code with confidence, fostering a culture of reliability and efficiency.

The chapter continued by addressing various types of tests, each serving a distinct purpose in the realm of software testing. We deciphered the nuances between unit tests, acceptance tests, and integration tests, employing a theatrical analogy to simplify these concepts.

Next, we navigated the intricacies of Pester files and their structures. Understanding the anatomy of these files laid the groundwork for crafting well-organized and potent tests. We also explored Pester's naming conventions and file structures, emphasizing the importance of clear categorization for different test types. This structuring ensures that tests are always in harmony with the code they validate.

This chapter provided a comprehensive foundation for the Pester journey ahead. By comprehending the core concepts of Pester, including its purpose, types of tests, and file structures, you are equipped with the foundational knowledge required to harness the full potential of this powerful testing framework.

In Chapter 2, we will focus on the key building blocks of Pester: **Describe**, **Context**, and **It**. These constructs provide the framework for structuring tests effectively, enabling us to validate different aspects of our scripts with precision. Let's get cracking!

CHAPTER 2

Mastering Pester Fundamentals

Welcome to the heart of Pester! In this chapter, we will delve deep into the fundamental building blocks that empower Pester to work its magic in the world of PowerShell testing. Understanding these core elements – **Describe**, **Context**, **It**, **BeforeAll**, **AfterAll**, **BeforeEach**, and **AfterEach** – is akin to mastering the essential chords in music or the basic strokes in painting. They form the foundation upon which your Pester tests will stand strong and resilient.

We will demystify the structure and purpose of these elements, guiding you through their application. By the end of this chapter, you'll not only comprehend the syntax and usage of Pester's fundamental components but also grasp their significance in crafting robust and reliable tests for your PowerShell scripts. So, let's embark on this journey of mastering Pester fundamentals, where you will gain the skills needed to wield the testing power of Pester effectively.

Understanding Blocks in Pester

In the realm of Pester, every test script revolves around a fundamental structure comprising various special script blocks. Each of these blocks plays a specific role, some obligatory and others optional. Let's start by unraveling the very cornerstone of a Pester test: the **Describe** block.

© Owen Heaume 2024
O. Heaume, *Getting Started with Pester 5*, https://doi.org/10.1007/979-8-8688-0306-2_2

Describe: The Pillar of Logical Organization

The **Describe** block stands as the foundational element, a compulsory presence in every Pester test. Its primary purpose is to encapsulate your tests within a coherent, logical group. Think of it as the opening act in a play, setting the stage for the performances to follow. This block fosters clarity and unity, making your tests not only functional but also visually organized.

Within the **Describe** block, you have the flexibility to nest other **Describe** blocks, although this practice is less common. Instead, there are more refined methods to create subgroups within your tests which we will explore shortly.

Furthermore, the **Describe** block can house any number of **Context** or **It** blocks, essential components we'll also delve into shortly.

Syntax

```
Describe "Function Name" { }
```

Typically, the first **Describe** block encapsulates the name of the function being tested, offering a clear context for the ensuing tests. For instance,

```
Describe "Get-User" {
    # Code continues here
}
```

Beyond its fundamental structure, the **Describe** block supports various parameters, some of which we'll explore in more depth later in this book.

Understanding the nuances of the **Describe** block lays the foundation for well-organized and comprehensible Pester tests.

Next, we will uncover its sibling components – **Context** and **It** blocks – each adding a layer of specificity and detail to your tests.

Context: Adding Contextual Relevance

While **Describe** blocks create overarching categories, **Context** blocks add contextual relevance. They enable you to define specific scenarios within a **Describe** block. Think of a **Context** block as an act within the aforementioned play, breaking down the drama into distinct scenes.

Like the **Describe** block, it also supports several other parameters we'll see later; however, unlike the **Describe** block, **Context** blocks are optional, and you can choose to use them or not. If you do use them, you can have any number of them nested within your Describe block.

Syntax

```
Context "Scenario Description" { }
```

Listing 2-1 shows how you might use **Context** blocks.

Listing 2-1. Using multiple Context blocks for added clarity

```
Describe "Get-User" {
    Context "When User Exists" {
        # Tests for scenarios where user exists go here
    }

    Context "When User Doesn't Exist" {
        # Tests for scenarios where user doesn't exist go here
    }
}
```

It: Defining Specific Tests

At the heart of your Pester tests are the **It** blocks. These mandatory blocks define specific tests, encapsulating individual assertions about your code's behavior. Each **It** block represents a unique test case, akin to pivotal moments within an act, providing detailed information about the unfolding drama.

Syntax

```
It "Specific Test Description" { }
```

Listing 2-2 demonstrates *It* blocks in action.

Listing 2-2. Each It block represents a test case for your code

```
Describe "Get-User" {
    Context "When User Exists" {
        It "Should Retrieve User Information" {
            # Specific test assertions go here
        }

        It "Should Return User's Full Name" {
            # More test assertions go here
        }
    }
}
```

Understanding the roles of **Describe**, **Context**, and **It** blocks is akin to mastering the grammar of a language. With these foundational elements, you can articulate precise, reliable, and informative tests for your PowerShell scripts. In the upcoming sections, we'll explore these blocks in greater depth, unveiling their nuances and best practices. Let's continue our exploration, building the expertise needed to wield the full power of Pester in your testing endeavors by looking at four other optional script blocks.

Setting the Stage with BeforeAll

In Pester, preparing the ground for your tests is crucial. That's where the **BeforeAll** block steps in. This specialized script block acts as a backstage manager, ensuring everything is in order before the main performance begins. Here's a closer look at how it operates.

The nonmandatory **BeforeAll** block is designed to handle preconditions necessary for your **Describe** or **Context** blocks. It executes once for the entire **Describe** or **Context** and runs only once, providing an efficient way to initialize essential elements for your tests.

The **BeforeAll** block can be used to set up anything your subsequent tests will require as a one-time operation, be that initializing variables to creating objects. Commonly, the **BeforeAll** block is used to import the function under scrutiny by dot sourcing it, setting the stage for subsequent tests. Here's an example of its usage at different levels:

At the Container Level

```
BeforeAll {
    # Dot source the function to be tested
}

Describe "Get-User" {
    # Tests go here
}
```

At the Describe or Context Level

```
Describe "Get-User" {
    BeforeAll {
        # Set up specific conditions for this
        # Describe or Context
        $Name = "Owen"
    }

    It "Should Test Something" {
        # Test using the initialized conditions
        Get-User -Name $Name
    }
}
```

In this way, the **BeforeAll** block acts as the backstage crew, ensuring a smooth performance for your tests by handling the necessary setup before the curtain rises.

Clearing the Stage with AfterAll

In the intricate theater of Pester testing, the performance isn't truly over until the stage is spotless. Enter the **AfterAll** block, akin to the dedicated crew that tidies up after the grand spectacle. This nonmandatory specialized script block ensures a seamless cleanup operation after all the tests have had their moment in the spotlight.

The **AfterAll** block is your backstage cleanup crew, responsible for removing any traces left behind after the tests have run their course. Just as the **BeforeAll** block sets the stage, the **AfterAll** block ensures that the stage is left pristine, ready for the next act. It executes once, after all the tests in the **Describe** or **Context** block have concluded, providing a singular opportunity to perform essential cleanup tasks.

Imagine this scenario: your tests create temporary files or databases to simulate real-world conditions. The **BeforeAll** block sets the scene, while the **AfterAll** block, much like a diligent cleaning crew, sweeps away these temporary constructs, leaving your system in a pristine state. Listing 2-3 shows an example of the **AfterAll** block in action.

Listing 2-3. The AfterAll block

```
BeforeAll {
    # Code to set up resources for testing
    New-Item -Path C:\Temp\TestFile.txt -ItemType File
}

Describe "Sample Test Suite" {
    It "Should do something" {
        # Test code
    }
```

```
    # More tests...

}

AfterAll {
        # Code to clean up resources after testing
        Remove-Item -Path C:\Temp\TestFile.txt -Force
}
```

In this scenario, the **BeforeAll** block stages the necessary resources, and the **AfterAll** block ensures a meticulous cleanup, *even if some acts didn't go as planned* (i.e., some of the tests failed), leaving the testing environment as pristine as it was before the performance began. With the **AfterAll** block in place, your tests conclude with a flourish, leaving no trace of their existence behind.

Preparing the Ground with BeforeEach

When testing, consistency and reliability are paramount. The show must go on smoothly, regardless of the number of acts or performers. That's where the **BeforeEach** block takes its cue, ensuring that every act is set up perfectly before it takes the stage. Let's explore its crucial role in the Pester performance.

The **BeforeEach** block acts as the backstage crew of your tests, diligently preparing the stage for each individual performance. It executes once before every **It** block within the current **Context** or **Describe** block.

Since **It** blocks are where the actual tests unfold, the **BeforeEach** block ensures that whatever is contained within its script block is executed right before each test. For example, if you have two **It** blocks within your **Describe** block, the **BeforeEach** block will execute twice, once for each **It**.

This block is commonly used to create prerequisites for the current tests. Whether it's initializing variables, setting up mock functions, or establishing connections, the **BeforeEach** block guarantees that each test starts on a level playing field, ensuring consistent and reliable outcomes.

Here's an example of its implementation:

```
Describe "Testing Something" {
    BeforeEach {
        # Setup code here
    }

    It "should perform a specific task" {
        # Test code here
    }

    It "should handle another task" {
        # Test code here
    }
}
```

BeforeEach executes before any block within the current block or any of its child blocks. To illustrate, consider Listing 2-4, where the **BeforeEach** block will run before "Test1," "Test2," and "Test3," ensuring each one starts on a level playing field.

Listing 2-4. BeforeEach in Action

```
Describe "Scope Test" {
    BeforeEach {
        # Code for setting up the stage
        Write-host "I run before each test"
    }

    It "test1" {

        Write-Host "Test1"
    }
```

```
Context "The Context block" {

    It "Test2" {

        Write-Host "Test2"
    }
    It "test3" {

        Write-Host "Test3"
    }
  }
}
```

Running Listing 2-4 presents the following output as shown in Figure 2-1.

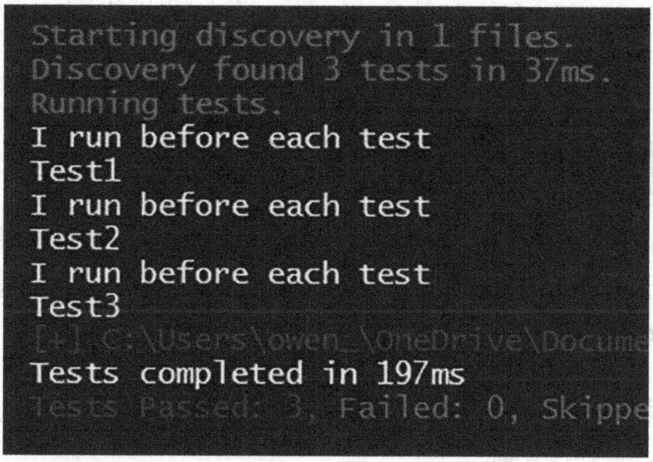

Figure 2-1. *The Write-Host output runs before every test*

In this way, the **BeforeEach** block ensures that each test begins its performance with the same meticulously prepared stage, leading to a consistent and flawless Pester production.

Nurturing Cleanliness with AfterEach

In the world of testing, ensuring a pristine environment after every trial is as crucial as the test itself. Enter **AfterEach**, your trusted cleanup crew in the Pester theater. Just as **BeforeEach** sets the stage, **AfterEach** ensures that the stage is left spotless after each performance, providing a fresh start for every subsequent test.

Much like its counterpart **BeforeEach**, **AfterEach** possesses the same attributes and operates with similar precision. **AfterEach** diligently follows every individual test within its current block or any of its child blocks. It's akin to a diligent janitor, swiftly tidying up the aftermath of each test, ensuring no residue is left behind.

By cleaning up any resources or setups used during the tests, **AfterEach** maintains the integrity of your testing environment. Imagine it as a backstage team ensuring that every prop is back in its place and every costume is neatly hung after each act.

Note   Like its counterpart, **AfterAll**, **AfterEach** will run even if a test fails, guaranteeing test cleanup!

Listing 2-5 demonstrates AfterEach via Write-Host statements to show the execution flow.

Listing 2-5. AfterEach will run after each test

```
Describe "Scope Test" {
    AfterEach {
        # Code for setting up the stage
        Write-host "I run after each test"
    }
```

```
It "test1" {

    Write-Host "Test1"
}
Context "The Context block" {

    It "Test2" {

        Write-Host "Test2"
    }
    It "test3" {

        Write-Host "Test3"
    }
}
}
```

Running Listing 2-5 results in the following output as shown in Figure 2-2.

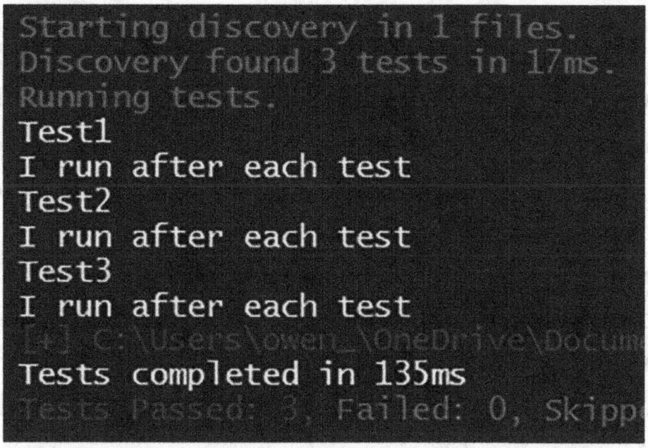

Figure 2-2. *The results of AfterEach*

In the grand play of testing, **AfterEach** ensures that the stage is reset to its original state, ready for the next captivating performance.

Summary

In this chapter, we navigated through the foundational elements that empower Pester. These essential building blocks, including Describe, Context, It, BeforeAll, AfterAll, BeforeEach, and AfterEach, serve as the fundamental chords in the symphony of Pester, forming the robust foundation for crafting reliable tests.

We unraveled the structure and purpose of each element, emphasizing their significance in creating tests for PowerShell scripts. By the chapter's end, readers not only gained a comprehensive understanding of the syntax and usage of these components but also grasped their role in building resilient and effective tests.

The chapter commenced with a focus on the Describe block, the pillar of logical organization in Pester tests. Analogous to the opening act in a play, it sets the stage for performances by encapsulating tests within coherent, logical groups. We explored its syntax and nuances, laying the groundwork for the subsequent exploration of its siblings – Context and It blocks.

Context blocks were introduced as tools to add contextual relevance, breaking down the drama into distinct scenes within a Describe block. Their optional nature and ability to nest within Describe blocks were highlighted, providing readers with a deeper understanding of their role in structuring tests.

The heart of Pester tests, the It block, was then spotlighted. As mandatory components, It blocks define specific tests, encapsulating individual assertions about code behavior. Each It block represents a unique test case, contributing to the detailed narrative of the script's performance.

Moving beyond these foundational elements, we explored four optional script blocks – BeforeAll, AfterAll, BeforeEach, and AfterEach – each playing a crucial role in orchestrating the testing performance.

BeforeAll, acting as the backstage manager, prepares the ground for tests, executing once for the entire Describe or Context. It is a powerful tool for initializing essential elements for subsequent tests, ensuring a smooth performance.

AfterAll, the backstage cleanup crew, ensures a seamless cleanup operation after all tests in the Describe or Context block have concluded. It removes any traces left behind, leaving the testing environment pristine for subsequent acts.

BeforeEach, likened to the backstage crew, diligently prepares the stage for each individual performance. Executing before every It block within the current Context or Describe, it ensures consistent and reliable outcomes by setting up prerequisites for each test.

AfterEach, similar to BeforeEach, operates as a cleanup crew. It maintains the integrity of the testing environment by swiftly tidying up after each test, ensuring a fresh start for subsequent performances.

With these fundamental elements and their detailed exploration, readers are equipped to harness the full power of Pester in their testing endeavors. The chapter provided not only syntax insights but also practical examples, directing readers toward mastering the essentials of Pester.

Chapter 3 awaits, guiding you through the practical aspects of Pester testing.

Writing Your First Tests

With a solid understanding of the fundamental concepts, it's time to roll up your sleeves and start writing your first Pester tests. But before we dive into the practical aspects, let's familiarize ourselves with some essential Pester cmdlets.

Pester Cmdlets

Pester, the PowerShell testing framework, features a collection of 28 cmdlets, including two aliases, as depicted in Figure 3-1. You will find yourself concentrating on approximately 13 or 14 of these cmdlets initially, streamlining the learning process. That's under half the available cmdlets and very manageable!

```
Administrator: Windows PowerShell
PS C:\> Get-Command -Module Pester

CommandType     Name                                  Version    Source
-----------     ----                                  -------    ------
Alias           Add-AssertionOperator                 5.5.0      Pester
Alias           Get-AssertionOperator                 5.5.0      Pester
Function        Add-ShouldOperator                    5.5.0      Pester
Function        AfterAll                              5.5.0      Pester
Function        AfterEach                             5.5.0      Pester
Function        Assert-MockCalled                     5.5.0      Pester
Function        Assert-VerifiableMock                 5.5.0      Pester
Function        BeforeAll                             5.5.0      Pester
Function        BeforeDiscovery                       5.5.0      Pester
Function        BeforeEach                            5.5.0      Pester
Function        Context                               5.5.0      Pester
Function        ConvertTo-JUnitReport                 5.5.0      Pester
Function        ConvertTo-NUnitReport                 5.5.0      Pester
Function        ConvertTo-Pester4Result               5.5.0      Pester
Function        Describe                              5.5.0      Pester
Function        Export-JUnitReport                    5.5.0      Pester
Function        Export-NUnitReport                    5.5.0      Pester
Function        Get-ShouldOperator                    5.5.0      Pester
Function        InModuleScope                         5.5.0      Pester
Function        Invoke-Pester                         5.5.0      Pester
Function        It                                    5.5.0      Pester
Function        Mock                                  5.5.0      Pester
Function        New-Fixture                           5.5.0      Pester
Function        New-MockObject                        5.5.0      Pester
Function        New-PesterConfiguration               5.5.0      Pester
Function        New-PesterContainer                   5.5.0      Pester
Function        Set-ItResult                          5.5.0      Pester
Function        Should                                5.5.0      Pester


PS C:\>
```

Figure 3-1. *The available Pester cmdlets*

To get a firm grip on their functionalities, I highly recommend investing 10 minutes to explore the help documentation for each cmdlet. You can do this by typing help <cmdlet> -full in a PowerShell window. Although some of these cmdlets will be explored in later chapters, for now, let's focus on three vital ones: **It**, **Should**, and **Get-ShouldOperator**.

It

The **It** command finds its home inside a **Describe** or **Context** block. If you're well acquainted with the AAA pattern (Arrange-Act-Assert), (if not then do not fret – we will go over this shortly), the body of the **It** block is where assertions should be placed.

The convention here is to have one clear expectation per **It** block. Any code inside the **It** block should throw a terminating error if the test's expectation isn't met, subsequently causing the test to fail. The name of the **It** block should explicitly express what the test is expecting.

The **It** block follows this structure:

```
It "tests something" { }
```

Should

In addition to creating your own logic for testing expectations and throwing exceptions, Pester also provides the **Should** command, allowing you to perform assertions in plain language.

Should is a keyword specifically used to define assertions within an **It** block. It offers assertion methods to validate expectations, such as comparing objects. If an assertion isn't met, the test fails, and an exception is thrown.

You can use **Should** multiple times within an **It** block if you have more than one assertion to verify. Each **Should** keyword should be on a separate line, and the test will only pass if *all* assertions are met.

Get-ShouldOperator

Get-ShouldOperator returns a list of available Should parameters, their aliases, and examples to help you craft the tests you need. Especially beneficial for beginners, you can leverage it as a convenient reminder of which parameters are permissible and which are not.

Figure 3-2 shows the output of **Get-ShouldOperator**.

```
Administrator: Windows PowerShell
PS C:\> get-shouldoperator

Name                                      Alias
----                                      -----
Be                                        EQ
BeExactly                                 CEQ
BeGreaterThan                             GT
BeLessOrEqual                             LE
BeIn
BeLessThan                                LT
BeGreaterOrEqual                          GE
BeLike
BeLikeExactly
BeNullOrEmpty
BeOfType                                  HaveType
BeTrue
BeFalse
Contain
Exist
FileContentMatch
FileContentMatchExactly
FileContentMatchMultiline
FileContentMatchMultilineExactly
HaveCount
HaveParameter
Match
MatchExactly                              CMATCH
Throw
InvokeVerifiable
Invoke
```

Figure 3-2. *A list of all the valid Should operators*

This knowledge will lay a strong foundation for you to start crafting your own Pester tests. Let's move forward and put these concepts into action using **It**, **Should** and a few should operators.

The Structure of a Test

At its core, a test comprises at least one **Describe** block and one **It** block, with the **It** block encapsulating the actual test logic. The fundamental syntax is demonstrated in Listing 3-1.

Listing 3-1. Basic test syntax

```
Describe "The function being tested" {
    it "tests something" {

    # The test goes here

    }
}
```

To illustrate, let's craft a sample test using a straightforward function, **Get-Boolean** (shown in Listing 3-2). This function returns either true or false based on the supplied parameter.

Listing 3-2. The Get-Boolean function to be tested

```
function Get-Boolean {
    param (
        [ValidateSet ('True','False')]
        $myBoolean
    )

    if ($myBoolean -eq 'True') {
        $true
```

```
    } else {
        $false
    }
}
```

Now, we can construct tests for this function, as demonstrated in Listing 3-3 with the test execution result shown in Figure 3-3.

Listing 3-3. Testing the function logic. It should return True

```
Describe "Get-Boolean" {
    it "returns true" {
        $expectedResult = Get-Boolean -myBoolean True

        $expectedResult | should -BeTrue
    }
}
```

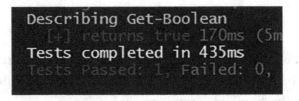

Figure 3-3. *The test result*

Testing True and False Scenarios

To expand our test coverage for the **Get-Boolean** function, we can introduce additional tests to verify its behavior for both true and false scenarios. In Listing 3-4, two tests are implemented.

Listing 3-4. Adding another test

```
Describe "Get-Boolean" {
    it "returns true" {
        $expectedResult = Get-Boolean -myBoolean True

        $expectedResult | should -BeTrue
    }

    it "returns false" {
        $expectedResult = Get-Boolean -myBoolean False

        $expectedResult | should -BeFalse
    }
}
```

In the first test, we ensure that the function returns true when provided with the parameter **True**. The **$expectedResult** is then piped to **Should -BeTrue** for assertion.

Conversely, the second test examines the behavior of the function when the parameter is set to **False**. The expected result is piped to **Should -BeFalse** for verification. Figure 3-4 shows the test results.

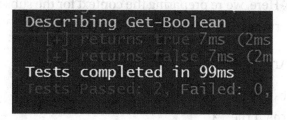

Figure 3-4. *The test results*

By incorporating these tests, we establish a more comprehensive examination of the **Get-Boolean** function, validating the function logic in both true and false scenarios. This approach aligns with the AAA pattern – Arranging the test, Acting on the code, and Asserting the expected outcome. As we progress, we'll explore more complex scenarios and assertions to fortify our testing practices.

The AAA Pattern: Arrange, Act, Assert

Adhering to a structured testing methodology enhances the clarity and effectiveness of your tests. The AAA pattern – Arrange, Act, and Assert – is a widely adopted approach in writing meaningful and maintainable tests.

Arrange

In the **Arrange** phase, you set up the necessary preconditions for your test. This includes initializing variables, defining inputs, and configuring the environment to mimic the conditions under which your code will run. This phase is crucial for isolating the specific functionality you want to test.

In the Listing 3-5, the creation of **$expectedResult** is part of the Arrange phase. Here, we're preparing the context for the subsequent action and assertion.

Listing 3-5. Arrange

```
Describe "Get-Boolean" {
    It "returns true" {
        # Arrange
        $expectedResult = Get-Boolean -myBoolean True

        $expectedResult | Should -BeTrue
    }
}
```

Act

The **Act** phase involves executing the specific functionality or code that you are testing. This is where you perform the actions that will produce the result you intend to evaluate as shown in Listing 3-6.

Listing 3-6. Act

```
Describe "Get-Boolean" {
    It "returns true" {
        # Arrange          # Act
        $expectedResult = Get-Boolean -myBoolean True

        $expectedResult | Should -BeTrue
    }
}
```

The invocation of **Get-Boolean -myBoolean True** represents the Act phase. We are triggering the function with a specific input to observe its behavior.

Assert

The **Assert** phase is where you verify the outcome of the executed code. It checks whether the actual result aligns with the expected result. In Pester, this is often done using the **Should** command with various operators as demonstrated in Listing 3-7.

Listing 3-7. Assert

```
Describe "Get-Boolean" {
    It "returns true" {
        # Arrange          # Act
        $expectedResult = Get-Boolean -myBoolean True
```

```
                    # Assert
        $expectedResult | Should -BeTrue
    }
}
```

In this example, **Should -BeTrue** is the assertion, confirming that the result obtained in the Act phase meets our expectations.

Adopting the AAA pattern provides a systematic and clear structure to your tests, making it easier to understand, maintain, and extend your test suite as your code evolves. To summarize AAA, let's relate it to the theater analogy used throughout this book so far.

The AAA Theater: A Pester Production

Imagine your test scenario as a theatrical performance – an intricate play unfolding on the stage of your development environment. In this theatrical setting, the AAA pattern takes center stage as the director, orchestrating a flawless performance.

Act 1: Arrange – Setting the Stage

The curtain rises on the **Arrange** phase, where actors (variables and environment setup) take their positions on the stage. Props are arranged, costumes are donned, and the scene is meticulously prepared. This is the moment when the backstage crew ensures that everything is ready for the upcoming act.

Act 2: Act – The Main Performance

As the lights focus on the main stage, the **Act** phase commences. The lead actors (your code) step forward, delivering their lines and executing their roles. The plot unfolds as the code comes to life, performing the actions that will shape the narrative of your test.

Act 3: Assert – The Grand Finale

The grand finale arrives in the **Assert** phase, akin to the climactic scene of the play. The audience (your test suite) eagerly awaits the resolution. Did the actors (code) deliver the expected performance? The assert phase is the critical moment of truth, where the success or failure of the production is revealed.

Just as a well-orchestrated theater production requires seamless coordination between the arrangement of actors, the execution of the play, and the final judgment of its success, the AAA pattern ensures a structured and effective performance in the theater of testing. Each act plays a vital role, contributing to the overall quality of the show. So, let the AAA Theater guide your testing endeavors, ensuring a standing ovation for your code.

A Glimpse into Should Operators

In our exploration of Pester's **Should** command, the diverse array of operators, as showcased earlier in Figure 3-2, might have caught your eye. While many of them are quite intuitive, a few might benefit from a bit more clarification. Let's delve into a couple of these operators.

-HaveParameter Operator

If your aim is to verify that your function boasts the expected parameters, then the **-HaveParameter** operator is your go-to. Consider our example function, **Get-Boolean**, which features a lone parameter, **$MyBoolean**. To ensure this parameter persists and hasn't undergone any unintended alterations in future code revisions, we can employ PowerShell's **Get-Command** cmdlet, as illustrated in Listing 3-8.

Listing 3-8. Testing for parameters

```
Describe Get-Boolean {
    It "Should contain the correct parameters" {
        Get-Command Get-Boolean | Should -HaveParameter
        "myBoolean"
    }
}
```

In this snippet, we assert that our function contains the **$MyBoolean**
parameter. Now, let's unpack what's happening here.

Explanation

1. **Get-Command Get-Boolean:** Utilizes the **Get-
    Command** cmdlet to retrieve information about the
    Get-Boolean function.

2. **Should -HaveParameter "myBoolean":** Employs
    the **-HaveParameter** operator to check whether
    the function includes the specified parameter,
    in this case, "myBoolean". (Note the quotes
    around **myBoolean** are optional, and there is no
    preceding "$".)

Note   If you wish to check that the function parameter is mandatory,
then add **-Mandatory** to the end of the assertion like so: Get-
Command Get-Boolean | Should -HaveParameter
-Mandatory

What Have We Accomplished?

By crafting this test, we've established a validation mechanism to ensure that the critical parameter, **$MyBoolean**, is intact within our function. This guards against accidental removal or renaming, contributing to the robustness and reliability of our code. In the broader context of your testing arsenal, leveraging operators like **-HaveParameter** adds precision to your tests, safeguarding the integrity of your functions as they evolve over time.

-BeOfType Operator

As we navigate the realm of Pester's **Should** command, the **-BeOfType** operator emerges as a valuable tool for verifying the type of object returned by a function. This proves especially handy when you want to ensure that your function delivers an object of a specific type, be it a string, a PSCustomObject, or another data type.

-BeOfType Operator in Action

Let's apply this operator to our familiar companion, the **Get-Boolean** function, which we know yields a Boolean result. In Listing 3-9, we craft a test to confirm this expected outcome.

Listing 3-9. Should Operator -BeOfType

```
Describe Get-Boolean {
    It " Should contain the correct parameters" {
        $expectedResult = Get-Boolean -myBoolean True

        $expectedResult | Should -BeOfType Bool
    }
}
```

Explanation

1. **$expectedResult = Get-Boolean -myBoolean True:** Invokes the **Get-Boolean** function, capturing its result in the **$expectedResult** variable.

2. **$expectedResult | Should -BeOfType Bool**: Uses the -BeOfType operator to assert that the type of the result stored in **$expectedResult** is indeed a Boolean.

A Note on Syntax Following **-BeOfType**, you have flexibility in specifying the data type. In this instance, we use "Bool" to indicate a Boolean type. Alternatively, you could employ "Boolean," "system. Boolean," or even "[System.Boolean]" – all achieving the same validation.

What Have We Accomplished?

This test ensures that the **Get-Boolean** function adheres to its expected behavior by returning a result of the correct data type. Verifying the type of output becomes crucial as it adds an extra layer of certainty to the function's performance. With **-BeOfType** and similar operators in your arsenal, you establish a robust defense against unexpected changes in your code's behavior. As our exploration advances, we'll continue to uncover additional operators that enhance the precision and reliability of your tests.

Running Your Tests

Writing tests is one thing, but executing them is the crucial next step in ensuring the reliability of your code. Let's explore a couple of methods to set your tests in motion.

Inline Execution

The simplest method involves embedding your tests directly within the script containing the functions under examination. In this approach, tests follow the functions they scrutinize, as demonstrated in Listing 3-10.

Listing 3-10. Inline testing

```
function Get-Boolean {
    param (
        [ValidateSet ('True','False')]
        $myBoolean
    )

    if ($myBoolean -eq 'True') {
        $true
    } else {
        $false
    }
}

Describe Get-Boolean {
    It " Should contain the correct parameters" {
        $expectedResult = Get-Boolean -myBoolean True

        $expectedResult | Should -BeOfType Bool
    }
}
```

Dot Sourcing

Another strategy involves segregating each function into its individual file, such as MyFunction1.ps1 and MyFunction2.ps1. With dot sourcing, you can then incorporate the functions and tests for execution, as illustrated in Listing 3-11.

Listing 3-11. Dot sourcing the function

```
BeforeAll {
    . $PSCommandPath.Replace('.Tests.ps1', '.ps1')
}

Describe Get-Boolean {
    It " Should contain the correct parameters" {
        $expectedResult = Get-Boolean -myBoolean True

        $expectedResult | Should -BeOfType Bool
    }
}
```

Decoding the BeforeAll Section

The BeforeAll block plays a pivotal role in the dot sourcing method. Specifically, it ensures the execution of the script containing the functions before the tests commence. Here, **$PSCommandPath** comes into play, containing the full path and name of the script that is currently being run. Of course, your .tests file needs to be located in the same directory as the function script being tested, or it won't work.

In the context of Listing 3-11, this path is manipulated to replace '.Tests.ps1' with '.ps1,' ensuring that the correct script is sourced before the tests are initiated.

Feel free to dot source the functions any way you like if you prefer to use `. $PSScriptRoot/myFunction.ps1` or a more long-winded method then go ahead.

Caution   Ensure that you wrap the dot source command within the **BeforeAll** script block; otherwise, it won't work.

If your function.ps1 file is in a different location to your .tests, you could still dot source it by explicitly naming the path like this:

```
BeforeAll {
    $scriptPath = "C:\Path\To\Your\Script.ps1
    . $scriptPath
}
```

This careful orchestration guarantees that the functions are seamlessly integrated into the testing environment, setting the stage for comprehensive evaluations.

Import-Module

When working with PowerShell modules and aiming to test the functions encapsulated within them, the process involves importing the module before executing the tests. This method proves invaluable for assessing the behavior and correctness of functions within the modular structure of your scripts.

In the following example, presented in Listing 3-12, we showcase how to seamlessly import a module to facilitate testing. This becomes particularly relevant when your script is organized into modular components, and you want to test each function's functionality independently.

Listing 3-12. Importing the module before tests

```
BeforeAll {
    $moduleName = 'yourModuleName'
    Get-Module -Name $moduleName -All | Remove-Module -Force
    $module = Get-Module -Name $moduleName -ListAvailable
    Import-Module -Name $module -Force
}

Describe "A function in the module" {
    It "tests something" {
        # test code
    }
}
```

Note   It's crucial to recognize that with this approach, you can exclusively test functions that have been exposed publicly by the module. This won't work for private functions, and we'll address this later in the book.

Decoding the BeforeAll Section

The **BeforeAll** block plays a crucial role in the process of importing modules. In this context, it ensures the designated module, identified by 'yourModuleName,' is removed and then imported before the tests begin. This guarantees a clean slate for testing the specific module functions.

Integrating Testing into Your Workflow

By embracing different execution methods, you gain the flexibility to seamlessly integrate testing into your development workflow. Whether you opt for the straightforward approach of inline execution, leverage the organizational advantages of dot sourcing, or harness the modular structure by importing modules, the decision is entirely yours. Each method caters to various preferences and project requirements.

Invoke the Magic

While it's convenient to press the "play," "execute," or "Run Script" button in your chosen IDE to run tests, consider leveraging the power of the **Invoke-Pester** command for a more insightful experience.

Executing tests through **Invoke-Pester** offers a deeper understanding of the various structures of your tests. For instance, if you opt for the traditional "run scripts" method or press F5 in the integrated Windows PowerShell IDE, you'll receive an output similar to what's shown in Figure 3-5.

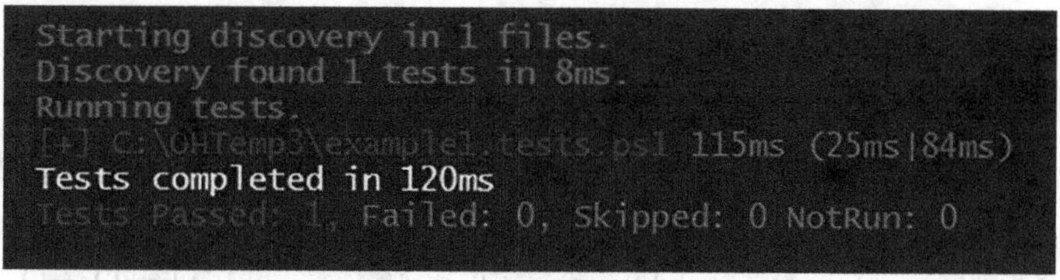

Figure 3-5. *Basic test output*

However, using **Invoke-Pester** introduces a wealth of parameters, including the powerful **-Output** option. When set to "detailed," this parameter transforms the output significantly, providing a more comprehensive test analysis, as illustrated in Figure 3-6 for the same set of tests.

```
PS C:\ohtemp3> invoke-pester -Path .\example1.tests.ps1 -Output Detailed
Pester v5.5.0

Starting discovery in 1 files.
Discovery found 1 tests in 24ms.
Running tests.

Running tests from 'C:\ohtemp3\example1.tests.ps1'
Describing Get-Greeting
 Context when testing the function
   [+] should return expected output 33ms (13ms|20ms)
Tests completed in 143ms
Tests Passed: 1, Failed: 0, Skipped: 0 NotRun: 0
```

Figure 3-6. Detailed output. Use the -Path parameter to point to the .tests.ps1 file location

Now, you can visualize a detailed breakdown of the different blocks the tests have passed through.

In later chapters, we'll delve into some of the other valuable parameters offered by **Invoke-Pester**.

Summary

In this chapter, you embarked on the practical journey of writing your initial Pester tests, laying a foundation for robust and reliable PowerShell scripts. You explored essential Pester cmdlets, focusing on It, Should, and Get-ShouldOperator. The chapter delved into the fundamental structure of a test, featuring the Describe and It blocks, and illustrated the process with a sample test for the Get-Boolean function.

The AAA pattern – Arrange, Act, and Assert – emerged as a guiding principle for structuring tests systematically. Through theatrical analogies, the chapter compared testing phases to a well-orchestrated play, emphasizing the importance of setting the stage, executing the main performance, and delivering a grand finale.

The introduction of two vital Should operators, -HaveParameter and -BeOfType, added precision to your tests. You explored testing parameters' existence and validating object types, enhancing the reliability of your scripts.

Execution methods, including inline execution, dot sourcing, and module importing, were thoroughly examined. Each method was explained, decoded, and contextualized within the broader framework of integrating testing into your development workflow.

Additionally, the chapter touched upon the power of Invoke-Pester, providing a deeper insight into test structures and paving the way for a more comprehensive understanding of your script's performance.

In Chapter 4, you will delve into the nuanced world of block scope within Pester. Understanding how variables and scopes behave in different blocks is crucial for writing effective and maintainable tests. As you master block scope in Pester, you'll gain insights that elevate your testing practices, contributing to the overall excellence of your PowerShell scripts. Get ready to enhance your skills and refine your testing prowess in the upcoming chapter!

CHAPTER 4

Mastering Block Scope in Pester

As we journey through Pester testing, mastering the concept of block scope is paramount for ensuring the accuracy and reliability of your tests. This chapter delves deep into the intricacies of block scope, unraveling its nuances and clarifying its importance in Pester scripting. Through meticulous examination and hands-on exploration, we will navigate the terrain of block scope, providing you with the insights and understanding necessary to craft robust and precise tests in Pester.

Defining Block Scope

Consider our illustrative function, **Get-Greeting** (Listing 4-1), designed to greet users based on their names.

Listing 4-1. The function being tested

```
function Get-Greeting {
    param (
        [string]$Name
    )

    if ($name -eq "Owen") {
        write-host "Hello $name" -ForegroundColor green
```

© Owen Heaume 2024
O. Heaume, *Getting Started with Pester 5*, https://doi.org/10.1007/979-8-8688-0306-2_4

```
        return 5
    } elseif ($name -eq "Judith") {
        write-host "Hello, Judith" -ForegroundColor Cyan
        return 6
    } else {
        write-host "Who are you?" -ForegroundColor Magenta
        return 7
    }
}
```

When testing this function with Pester (Listing 4-2), you encounter an issue: the variable **$myvar**, declared in the Arrange phase within the first **It** block, is invisible to subsequent blocks within the same context, causing a test failure.

Listing 4-2. The second test will fail

```
Describe "Get-Greeting" {
    context "testing" {

        It "Returns expected output" {

            # Arrange
            $myvar = 5

            # Act
            $expected = Get-Greeting -Name 'Owen'

            # Assert
            $expected | Should -Be $myvar

        }
```

```
it "will fail" {

    # Assert
    $myvar | should -be 5

    }

  }

}
```

In Figure 4-1 you can see the results of the Pester test – note the second test has failed.

```
Describing Get-Greeting
  Context testing
Hello Owen
    [+] Returns expected output 15ms (
    [-] will fail 6ms (5ms|1ms)
    Expected 5, but got $null.
    at $myvar | should -be 5, C:\User
    at <ScriptBlock>, C:\Users\owen_\
Tests completed in 134ms
Tests Passed: 1, Failed: 1, Skipped:

PS C:\Users\owen_\OneDrive\Documents\
```

Figure 4-1. *The second test failed because of a scoping issue*

Elevating Scope with BeforeAll

To grant accessibility of **$myvar** to all **It** blocks within the context, you can employ the **BeforeAll** block, as demonstrated in Listing 4-3.

Importantly, **BeforeAll** will now apply to all child blocks of the context level, ensuring the smooth execution of tests and underscoring the necessity of defining code elements at appropriate scope levels.

By defining **BeforeAll** at the Context level, any code elements within it become visible to all tests within that context.

Listing 4-3. Moving BeforeAll to the Context block

```
Describe "Get-Greeting" {
    context "testing" {

        BeforeAll {
            $myvar = 5
        }

        It "Returns expected output" {

            # Act
            $expected = Get-Greeting -Name 'Owen'

            # Assert
            $expected | Should -Be $myvar

        }
        it "will pass" {

            # Assert
            $myvar | should -be 5

        }
    }
}
```

With the scope changed, the tests both pass as shown in Figure 4-2.

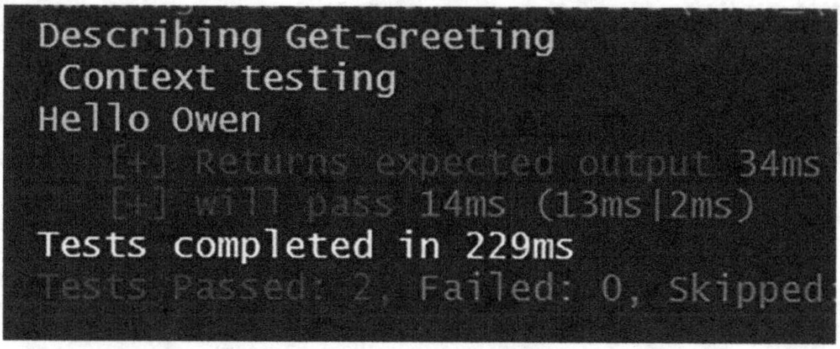

Figure 4-2. *All tests now pass*

Note   Keen-eyed readers might have noticed the somewhat unattractive inclusion of "Hello Owen" within the test output. Fear not, for this less-than-ideal embellishment in the test results can be effortlessly addressed. Further insights into this matter will unfold in the forthcoming chapter dedicated to the art of mocking.

Contextual Hierarchies and Limitations

Navigating through different contexts reveals a crucial aspect of block scope: **BeforeAll** is inherited only by child scopes of its context. Listing 4-4 demonstrates this: the test within the second context block will fail.

Listing 4-4. Tests in the second Context block will fail

```
Describe "Get-Greeting" {
    context "testing" {

        BeforeAll {
            $myvar = 5
        }
```

```
It "Returns expected output" {

    # Act
    $expected = Get-Greeting -Name 'Owen'

    # Assert
    $expected| Should -Be $myvar

}

it "will pass" {

    # Assert
    $myvar | should -be 5

}
}

Context "something else" {

    it "will fail" {

        # Assert
        $myvar | should -be 5
    }
}
}
```

In Figure 4-3, you can see that the test within the second context block
has failed.

```
Describing Get-Greeting
 Context testing
Hello Owen
   [+] Returns expected output  23ms
   [+] will pass  9ms  (6ms|3ms)
 Context something else
   [-] will fail  8ms  (5ms|4ms)
   Expected 5, but got $null.
   at $myvar | should -be 5, C:\Us
   at <ScriptBlock>, C:\Users\owen
Tests completed in 167ms
Tests Passed: 2, Failed: 1, Skipped
```

Figure 4-3. *Oh no – an unexpected test failure due to scope definition*

To broaden the variable's scope across all contexts, you move the **BeforeAll** block to the parent scope, the **Describe** block, as shown in Listing 4-5. Now, every context (and its child blocks) within the **Describe** block has access to the top-level variables because the **BeforeAll** will apply to any and all child blocks of the **Describe** block.

Listing 4-5. BeforeAll has moved up a level. All tests now pass

```
Describe "Get-Greeting" {

    BeforeAll {
        $myvar = 5
    }

    context "testing" {

        It "Returns expected output" {
```

```
        # Act
        $expected = Get-Greeting -Name 'Owen'

        # Assert
        $expected | Should -Be $myvar

    }

    it "will pass" {

        # Assert
        $myvar | should -be 5

    }
}

Context "something else" {

    it "will pass" {

        # Assert
        $myvar | should -be 5

    }
}
}
```

After shifting the scope up a level, the tests now pass as expected as shown in Figure 4-4.

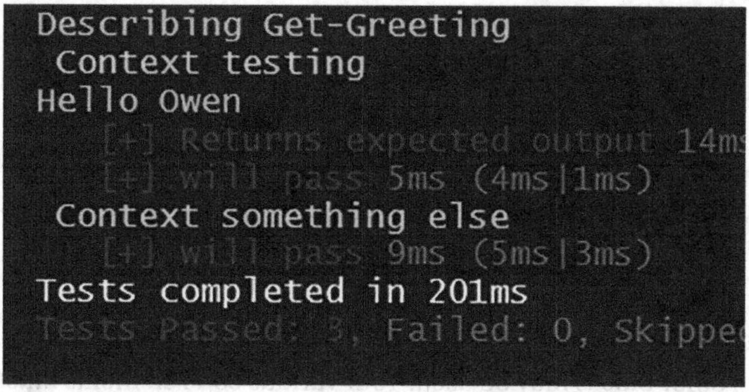

```
Describing Get-Greeting
  Context testing
Hello Owen
      [+] Returns expected output 14ms
      [+] will pass 5ms (4ms|1ms)
  Context something else
      [+] will pass 9ms (5ms|3ms)
Tests completed in 201ms
Tests Passed: 3, Failed: 0, Skipped
```

Figure 4-4. *The scope is in the Describe block and all tests pass*

The Perils of Unbounded Scope

Attempting to declare **$myvar** outside the allowed blocks as shown in Listing 4-6 leads to unexpected outcomes. All tests fail because **$myvar** has not been declared within a valid script block.

Listing 4-6. Doomed to failure

```
Describe "Get-Greeting" {
    context "testing" {

        $myvar = 5

    It "will fail" {

        # Act
        $expected = Get-Greeting -Name 'Owen'

        # Assert
        $expected| Should -Be $myvar

    }
```

```
    it "will also fail" {

        # Assert
        $myvar | should -be 5

    }

  }

}
```

In the code examples for this chapter, we have been using **BeforeAll** although other blocks may be used. Your various code elements *must* be encapsulated within designated script blocks, such as **It**, **BeforeAll**, **BeforeEach**, **AfterAll**, or **AfterEach**. Straying from these guidelines results in unpredictable behavior, as shown in Figure 4-5, emphasizing the importance of adhering to specified scopes.

```
Describing Get-Greeting
 Context testing
Hello Owen
    [-] will fail 15ms (10ms|5ms)
    Expected $null, but got 5.
    at $expected| Should -Be $myvar,
    at <ScriptBlock>, C:\Users\owen_\C
    [-] will also fail 7ms (6ms|1ms)
    Expected 5, but got $null.
    at $myvar | should -be 5, C:\Users
    at <ScriptBlock>, C:\Users\owen_\C
Tests completed in 200ms
Tests Passed: 0, Failed: 2, Skipped: 0
```

Figure 4-5. *All your code elements must be encapsulated within a valid script block. In Listing 4-6, $myvar has been declared in the context block but is not within its own script block, such as BeforeAll or BeforeEach, causing all tests to fail*

Our Ubiquitous Theater Analogy

In software testing, understanding block scope is akin to directing a multifaceted stage production. Each script block – be it **It**, **BeforeAll**, **BeforeEach**, **AfterAll**, or **AfterEach** – represents a distinct act in the play.

Within these acts, variables, commands, and other testing elements are performers, each playing a role crucial to the overall performance. The director (tester) ensures that every element, from simple variables to complex commands, understands their place and purpose within their designated acts.

Just as actors seamlessly transition between scenes, variables and commands flow flawlessly from one block to another, creating a cohesive and impactful testing narrative.

This orchestration ensures that when the curtains rise (tests run), the entire production unfolds with precision and effectiveness, leaving the audience (developers and stakeholders) in awe of the seamless performance on the testing stage.

Summary

In this chapter, we delved into the critical concept of block scope within Pester testing. The chapter meticulously explored the nuances of block scope, clarifying its intricacies and highlighting its pivotal role in crafting accurate and reliable tests. Through hands-on exploration, we navigated the landscape of block scope, offering insights and understanding to empower you in the creation of robust and precise Pester tests.

The journey began with the definition of block scope, using the illustrative function Get-Greeting to demonstrate the challenges posed by variable scope within Pester. The chapter emphasized the importance of defining code elements at appropriate scope levels for smooth test execution.

We explored the introduction of BeforeAll to elevate scope, ensuring variables are accessible to all It blocks within a context. The contextual hierarchies and limitations were uncovered, emphasizing the inheritance of BeforeAll only by child scopes of its context. The solution was presented by moving the BeforeAll block to the parent scope, the Describe block.

The chapter highlighted the perils of unbounded scope, illustrating the unexpected outcomes of declaring variables outside valid script blocks. The importance of encapsulating code elements within designated script blocks, such as It, BeforeAll, BeforeEach, AfterAll, or AfterEach, was underscored for predictable behavior.

Finally, our ubiquitous theater analogy portrayed understanding block scope as directing a multifaceted stage production. Each script block represented a distinct act, and variables and commands played crucial roles akin to performers. The director (tester) orchestrated a seamless flow of elements between acts, ensuring a cohesive and impactful testing narrative.

Next, in Chapter 5, we'll explore the efficiency of Pester's -ForEach parameter and delve into the world of data-driven testing, enhancing the scalability and readability of your Pester test suite.

CHAPTER 5

Data-Driven Tests

Efficiency in testing is not just about ensuring the functionality of individual components but also about managing your testing suite intelligently. As your PowerShell scripts evolve and diversify, you may encounter scenarios where numerous tests share a common structure or objective. Writing these tests individually can be time-consuming and may lead to redundancy in your codebase.

Drawing inspiration from the principles of data-driven testing, this chapter explores how to leverage the **-ForEach** parameter in Pester. We'll guide you through its application, demonstrating how it enables you to create concise and maintainable tests. By the end of this chapter, you'll not only understand the mechanics of **-ForEach** but also appreciate its role in enhancing the efficiency and readability of your Pester test suite.

Testing the Waters: Rigorous Evaluation of Remove-Files Functionality

In the journey of mastering Pester, we encounter scenarios where a function, like the illustrative **Remove-Files** in Listing 5-1, becomes a pivotal element of our PowerShell arsenal. This function adeptly deletes files based on specified parameters, showcasing the functionality that we want to subject to rigorous testing.

© Owen Heaume 2024

O. Heaume, *Getting Started with Pester 5*, https://doi.org/10.1007/979-8-8688-0306-2_5

Listing 5-1. Remove-Files – our sample function

```
function Remove-Files {

    param (
        [ValidateSet ('txt', 'log', 'tmp')]
        [string]$FileType,

        [Parameter(Mandatory = $true)]
        [string]$Path
    )

    switch ($FileType) {
        'txt' { Remove-Item -Path $Path\*.txt -Force }
        'log' { Remove-Item -Path $Path\*.log -Force }
        'tmp' { Remove-Item -Path $Path\*.tmp -Force }
    }
}
```

As diligent testers, we start by crafting tests for **Remove-Files**, as depicted in Listing 5-2. Each test focuses on a specific file type, ensuring our function behaves as expected.

Listing 5-2. Initial tests

```
Describe 'Remove-Files' {
    Context 'when removing files from the specified path' {
        It 'should remove all txt files' {
            Remove-Files -FileType 'txt' -Path 'C:\Temp'

            $files = Get-ChildItem -Path 'C:\Temp' ↵
            -Filter '*.txt'
            $files | Should -BeNullOrEmpty
        }
```

```
    it 'should remove all log files' {
        Remove-Files -FileType 'log' -Path 'C:\Temp'

        $files = Get-ChildItem -Path 'C:\Temp' ↵
        -Filter '*.log'
        $files | Should -BeNullOrEmpty
    }

    it 'should remove all tmp files' {
        Remove-Files -FileType 'tmp' -Path 'C:\Temp'

        $files = Get-ChildItem -Path 'C:\Temp' ↵
        -Filter '*.tmp'
        $files | Should -BeNullOrEmpty
    }
  }
}
```

Warning   It's essential to be aware that executing Listing 5-2 would result in the deletion of files. We plan to address this scenario in a later chapter. Kindly refrain from running this in a production environment or any environment where you want to keep your files!

Reviewing Chapter Insights with Listing 5-2

Before we proceed with adapting our test to embrace a data-driven approach, let's pause and reinforce our understanding of previous chapters by dissecting the details of Listing 5-2.

Describe 'Remove-Files'

This initiates a test suite or group named 'Remove-Files', providing a logical container for related tests.

Context 'when removing files from the specified path'

Within the 'Remove-Files' suite, there is a **context** defined. A **context** is a way to further organize tests within a suite based on specific scenarios or conditions. In this case, the context is 'when removing files from the specified path', indicating that the following tests will focus on the behavior of Remove-Files under this circumstance.

It 'should remove all txt files'

Inside the context, there is an individual test defined using the **It** statement. This test checks the behavior of the Remove-Files function when instructed to remove all '.txt' files from the 'C:\Temp' path.

```
Remove-Files -FileType 'txt' -Path 'C:\Temp'
$files = Get-ChildItem -Path 'C:\Temp' -Filter '*.txt'
$files | Should -BeNullOrEmpty
```

1. **Remove-Files -FileType 'txt' -Path 'C:\Temp':** This line calls the Remove-Files function with the parameters set to delete '.txt' files from the specified path.

2. **$files = Get-ChildItem -Path 'C:\Temp' -Filter '*.txt':** This line retrieves all '.txt' files in the 'C:\Temp' directory and assigns them to the variable $files.

3. **$files | Should -BeNullOrEmpty:** This line uses the Pester **Should** statement to assert that the $files variable should be null or empty. In other words, it checks that all '.txt' files have been successfully removed.

The subsequent tests for log and tmp files follow a similar structure, each verifying that the corresponding file types are removed from the specified path. The tests are organized hierarchically within the context, providing a clear structure for understanding and running tests related to file removal behavior in different scenarios.

Unlocking Efficiency: Data-Driven Testing with -ForEach in Pester

Now, let's explore the concept of data-driven tests in Pester. This methodology involves supplying a construct with an array of different input data sets, ensuring our code functions correctly across diverse scenarios. Typically implemented using **-ForEach** on an **It** block, this technique can also ascend to the **Describe** block level for data-driven tests on multiple **It** blocks within the **Describe** or **Context** blocks.

To leverage **-ForEach**, we structure the test data as an array of hashtables, as seen in the following example:

```
@(
    @{ key = 'value' }
    @{ key = 'value' }
    # etc
)
```

The -**ForEach** construct in Pester streamlines our testing approach by executing one test for each item in the specified array. In Listing 5-3, we utilize this feature to enhance the efficiency of our tests.

Listing 5-3. Using -ForEach for data-driven tests

```
Describe "Remove-Files" {
    Context "when removing files from the specified path" {
        It "should remove all the correct files" -foreach @(
                @{ FileType = 'txt'; Path = 'C:\Temp' }
                @{ FileType = 'log'; Path = 'C:\Temp' }
                @{ FileType = 'tmp'; Path = 'C:\Temp' }
            ) {

                $files = Get-ChildItem -Path $path ↳
                -Filter $filetype
                Remove-Files -FileType $filetype -Path $path

                $files | Should -BeNullOrEmpty
            }
        }
}
```

We leverage the capability to use multiple keys when creating array data. Specifically, in this instance, we employ two keys: **FileType** and **Path**. These keys correspond to the parameters of our function **Remove-Files** (you can name the keys according to your preference) forming the basis of our test data. It's important to note that each key-value pair is separated by a semi-colon in the array.

By implementing this approach, we consolidate our test code into a single block within the -**ForEach** construct. The array contains sets of data for three distinct tests, each representing a unique file type and path combination.

In this test structure, each key within the hashtable item serves as a variable in the test code. For instance, **$filetype** and **$path** used as parameters when calling the function **Remove-Files** represent the keys "filetype" and "path" in the hashtable, dynamically adapting to the associated values during each test execution. The test is run three times, once for each hashtable.

This consolidated test structure not only enhances the readability of our code but also promotes scalability. It simplifies the process of adding new test scenarios by extending the array with additional key-value sets, demonstrating the flexibility and power of data-driven testing in Pester.

Let's finish this section with our tried-and-tested theater analogy:

Imagine our testing journey as a theatrical production. The stage is set with a powerful concept – Data-Driven Testing with -ForEach in Pester. As the curtain rises, we explore the intricacies of this methodology, akin to supplying a stage with diverse props and settings. The star of our show, -ForEach, takes center stage in the 'It' block, but its performance extends to the grandeur of the 'Describe' block, orchestrating a symphony of tests across various scenarios.

In this theatrical script, our test data, elegantly structured as an array of hashtables, plays a crucial role. Each key and value in this array is like a well-rehearsed actor, ready to deliver a stellar performance. As the plot unfolds in Listing 5-3, the **-ForEach** construct takes its cue, executing tests with precision, enhancing the efficiency of our testing production.

Just like skilled actors adapting to different roles, our test code gracefully transforms. Variables such as **$filetype** and **$path**, representing the heart of our test data, dynamically adjust during each test execution. This consolidated test structure becomes the script that not only captivates with its readability but also showcases the scalability of our production. Adding new test scenarios is like introducing new characters, extending the array with additional key-value sets.

In this testing theater, the flexibility and power of data-driven testing in Pester take the spotlight, delivering a performance that resonates with efficiency and scalability.

Introduction to Templates in Pester

In our journey through Pester, the significance of crafting efficient and informative tests cannot be overstated. As we delve into the realm of data-driven testing with Pester's **-foreach** construct, we encounter scenarios where the output, while functional, lacks clarity. This brings us to the invaluable concept of templates, a tool that elevates the visibility and comprehensibility of our test results.

Templates Unveiled

When running data-driven tests, as demonstrated in Listing 5-3 previously, the output might leave us wanting more. While it informs us that tests were completed, the specifics of what each test evaluated remain elusive as shown in Figure 5-1.

```
Pester v5.5.0

Starting discovery in 1 files.
Discovery found 3 tests in 20ms.
Running tests.

Running tests from 'remove-files.tests.ps1'
Describing Remove-Files
  Context when removing files from the specified path
    [+] should remove all the correct files 174ms (14ms|160ms)
    [+] should remove all the correct files 10ms (7ms|3ms)
    [+] should remove all the correct files 6ms (4ms|2ms)
Tests completed in 458ms
Tests Passed: 3, Failed: 0, Skipped: 0 NotRun: 0
```

Figure 5-1. *Not overly helpful test results*

This is where templates come into play. In Pester, a template is defined by enclosing values within < >. For example, **<myValue>**, where Pester seamlessly expands these placeholders to their true values during test execution.

Utilizing Templates in Tests

Let's consider Listing 5-4, a refined version of our previous data-driven test. Here, we employ the template format < > to represent the hashtable's "FileType" and "Path" within the **It** description. **<FileType>** dynamically expands to the current hashtable FileType value and **<Path>** to the Path value.

Listing 5-4. Using templates for variable expansion

```
Describe "Remove-Files" {
    Context "when removing files from the specified path" {
        It "should remove all <FileType> files from <path>" ↩
        -foreach @(
                @{ FileType = 'txt'; Path = 'C:\Temp' }
                @{ FileType = 'log'; Path = 'C:\Temp' }
                @{ FileType = 'tmp'; Path = 'C:\Temp' }
            ) {

            $files = Get-ChildItem -Path $path ↩
            -Filter $filetype
            Remove-Files -FileType $filetype -Path $path

            $files | Should -BeNullOrEmpty
        }
    }
}
```

Figure 5-2 demonstrates running the test with templates, resulting in a clear and informative output.

```
Pester v5.5.0

Starting discovery in 1 files.
Discovery found 3 tests in 55ms.
Running tests.

Running tests from 'remove-files.tests.ps1'
Describing Remove-Files
  Context when removing files from the specified path
    [+] should remove all txt files from C:\Temp 37ms  (22ms|15ms)
    [+] should remove all log files from C:\Temp 8ms   (7ms|2ms)
    [+] should remove all tmp files from C:\Temp 6ms   (4ms|2ms)
Tests completed in 230ms
Tests Passed: 3, Failed: 0, Skipped: 0 NotRun: 0
```

Figure 5-2. *Using templates: resulting in a clear and informative output*

Expanding Template Scope

The beauty of templates lies in their versatility. While initially introduced in the context of **-foreach**, templates can extend beyond. In Listing 5-5, we showcase a valid use of templates outside a **-foreach** construct, where the variable **$response** is referenced within the **It** block description.

Listing 5-5. Any valid variable that is in-scope may be used in a template

```
Describe "MyFunction" {
    BeforeAll {
        $response = "Hello"
    }

    It "should respond with <response>" {
        # tests go here...
    }
}
```

The output of Listing 5-5 is a testament to the flexibility of templates as shown in Figure 5-3.

```
Pester v5.5.0

Starting discovery in 1 files.
Discovery found 1 tests in 42ms.
Running tests.

Running tests from 'remove-files.tests.ps1'
Describing MyFunction
  [+] should respond with Hello 17ms  (12ms|5ms)

Tests completed in 125ms
Tests Passed: 1, Failed: 0, Skipped: 0 NotRun: 0

PS C:\ohtemp4> |
```

Figure 5-3. *The template expands as expected*

A Note on Template Presentation

If you find the need to display < or > in your block descriptions without triggering template evaluation, simply escape each using the backtick, as illustrated in the following example:

```
It "Should `<not`> evaluate as a template" {
    # test code
}
```

When running the test, this results in a block description that reads as follows:

```
It "Should <not> evaluate as a template" {
    # test code
}
```

Templates in Pester not only enhance the readability of our code but also offer a powerful mechanism for scaling our tests, making them a valuable asset in our testing arsenal.

Summary

In this chapter, we delved into advanced Pester testing techniques, focusing on efficiency and scalability. Let's recap the key highlights of our exploration.

We introduced the crucial Remove-Files function, designed for targeted file deletion. Tests were crafted to thoroughly evaluate its functionality. A cautious approach was emphasized due to the impactful nature of Remove-Files in deleting files, paving the way for future enhancements.

We ventured into the realm of data-driven tests using Pester's -ForEach parameter. Test data was structured as an array of hashtables, enhancing test efficiency and readability. Multiple keys, such as FileType and Path, were leveraged to conduct tests across diverse scenarios within a consolidated structure.

Addressing the challenge of unclear output in data-driven tests, we introduced templates. Templates, defined with < >, dynamically expanded values in test descriptions, providing clarity. The versatility of templates was showcased beyond -ForEach, enriching the narrative of our testing script.

As this chapter concludes, your Pester toolkit has expanded, equipping you with advanced techniques for efficient and scalable testing. In Chapter 6, we'll delve into the intricacies of Pester's Discovery and Run phases, further refining your testing skills.

CHAPTER 6

Navigating the Pester Phases: Discovery and Run

Welcome to this chapter, where we delve into a thorough examination of the core phases that shape the Pester testing framework: Discovery and Run. Comprehending these phases is paramount for crafting impactful tests.

Our journey commences with a deep dive into Discovery, the stage where Pester discerns and readies the ground for testing. Following that, we seamlessly transition to the Run Phase, where the real performance materializes as tests are executed, and results assume the spotlight.

Prepare for an exploration into the inner workings of Pester's backstage, equipping you with the understanding required to proficiently navigate these indispensable testing phases.

Pester's Discovery Phase

Pester orchestrates its tests in two essential phases: **Discovery** and **Run**. The Discovery Phase kicks off the process by thoroughly scanning your test files, identifying **Describes**, **Contexts**, **Its**, and other critical Pester blocks that lay the groundwork for your tests; its purpose is to identify and categorize Pester blocks and tests.

© Owen Heaume 2024

O. Heaume, *Getting Started with Pester 5*, https://doi.org/10.1007/979-8-8688-0306-2_6

The Significance of Discovery

Discovery serves as the bedrock for various features in Pester 5 and sets the stage for potential advancements. Understanding why we adhere to certain practices during this phase is crucial for beginners. Let's dive deeper into the significance:

1. **Test Code Placement**

   - Constrain your test code within **It**, **BeforeAll**, **BeforeEach**, **AfterAll**, or **AfterEach** blocks to ensure a clear and structured organization of your tests.

   - **Why?** Placing test code within these specific blocks provides a logical structure to your tests. It helps Pester identify the scope and purpose of each block, making it easier to manage and execute tests selectively.

2. **Avoid Misplacement**

   - Any displaced code runs during Discovery, with results remaining elusive during the Run Phase, leading to confusion.

   - **Why?** During Discovery, Pester is scanning your script to identify and categorize various blocks and tests. Placing code outside the designated blocks can lead to unintended execution during Discovery, resulting in unexpected outcomes and difficulty in troubleshooting.

Illustrative Example

Consider the following script demonstrated in Listing 6-1.

Listing 6-1. Misplaced code outside of Pester blocks

```
# Misplaced code outside Pester blocks
Write-Host "This code runs during Discovery but may lead ⤷
to confusion."

Describe "PowerShell Wonders" {
    It "Performs Marvelous Feats" -ForEach @(
        @{ Action = "Sparkle"; Expected = 'Success'}
        @{ Action = "Thunder"; Expected = 'Powerful'}
    ) {
        Invoke-Wonder -Action $Action | Should -Be $Expected
    }
}

# More misplaced code outside Pester blocks
Write-Host "This code also runs during Discovery, ⤷
potentially causing unexpected outcomes."

Write-Host "Discovery Phases Completed."
```

In this example, all the **Write-Host** statements are placed outside the Pester blocks, violating the recommended practice. When running this script, the **Write-Host** statements will be executed during the Discovery Phase. Now, imagine these **Write-Host** statements were variables instead; any variable defined directly in the body of the script will be available during Discovery, but it won't be available during the important Run Phase. This can lead to confusion as these statements and variables might interfere with the intended setup or test execution.

It's crucial to confine code to the designated Pester blocks to ensure that it's executed in the appropriate context during the Run Phase and to avoid unexpected behaviors during the Discovery Phase.

Harnessing BeforeDiscovery

In certain scenarios where intentional code placement outside of Pester-controlled blocks is necessary, Pester provides a valuable script block: **BeforeDiscovery**. This special script block serves as a signaling mechanism to convey that specific code is intentionally placed outside the controlled leaf-blocks, such as on top of files or directly in the body of Describe/Context.

This becomes particularly relevant when dealing with dynamic code generation or setup activities that need to occur before Pester identifies and categorizes the various blocks and tests in your script.

Consider the following example shown in Listing 6-2, where **BeforeDiscovery** is utilized.

Listing 6-2. Using BeforeDiscovery

```
BeforeDiscovery {
    # Code intentionally placed outside Pester-controlled ⮡
    blocks to run during Discovery
    $scriptsToTest = Get-ChildItem -Path $PSScriptRoot ⮡
    -Filter '*.ps1' -Recurse
}

Describe "Script Validation - <_>" -ForEach $scriptsToTest ⮡
{
    Context "Code Structure" {
        It "Follows Best Practices" {
            # Test the script for adherence to coding ⮡
            standards
            # Example: Ensure proper indentation, naming ⮡
            conventions, etc.
        }

        It "Contains Proper Comments" {
```

```
# Test the script for the presence of meaningful ↵
comments
# Example: Ensure the inclusion of helpful ↵
comments for clarity
      }
    }
  }
}
```

Breaking Down the Magic

1. **BeforeDiscovery Block**

   – The **BeforeDiscovery** block houses code crucial for the Discovery Phase. This is where we strategically perform setup activities before Pester identifies and organizes tests. While it's technically possible to omit code from the **BeforeDiscovery** script block, adhering to Pester best practices and enhancing code readability is recommended. Essentially, we're affirming, "Yes, there is code outside of conventional script blocks, but it's intentionally placed here for a reason."

2. **Discovery Phase Dynamics**

   – As Pester journeys through the Discovery Phase, it evaluates the entire script, including the **BeforeDiscovery** block. This ensures that the code within **BeforeDiscovery** actively contributes to identifying and categorizing tests and setups.

   – All parameters provided to **It** are evaluated.

   – The **-ForEach** is evaluated.

   – The script block of **It** is saved but not executed. Tests are generated, one for each item in the **-foreach** array.

At the end of Discovery, Pester has collected all the tests and setups nestled within the script. These gems of information are securely stored in the internal data of the Pester module, ready for the spotlight in the upcoming Run Phase.

Tip   Note in the example Listing 6-2, we used the template **<_>**. **_** is the template equivalent of **$_,** which represents the current object.

This comprehension not only forms the bedrock of proficient testing practices but also guides us seamlessly into the next chapter of our exploration – the Run Phase, our dynamic companion in the realm of Pester.

Pester's Run Phase

In this section of our exploration of Pester phases, we transition from the Discovery Phase to the Run Phase. We will delve into the dynamic execution of tests, witnessing the real magic unfold. Understanding the Run Phase is vital for turning your PowerShell tests into actionable insights.

Run Phase Dynamics

While the Discovery Phase lays the groundwork, the Run Phase is where the action happens: Pester executes your tests based on the information gathered during Discovery. Let's unravel the dynamics of the Run Phase.

Execution Order Complexity

Pester version 5 introduces a more intricate execution order compared to its predecessor, Pester version 4. This complexity enhances the flexibility and capabilities of your test scripts but demands a deeper understanding. Let's break it down:

1. **Run the BeforeAll ScriptBlock**

    – Imports necessary modules or performs initial setup.

    – Establishes the foundation for the subsequent tests.

2. **Create New Scope**

    – Isolates the test from other tests.

    – Ensures a clean and independent execution environment.

3. **Invoke the It ScriptBlock**

    – Executes the first test within the isolated scope.

    – Validates the outcome based on the Should statement.

4. **Return to Previous Scope**

    – Steps back to the outer scope after completing the first test.

5. **Create New Scope (Again)**

    – Prepares the stage for the next test.

    – Maintains isolation between tests for consistent results.

6. **Invoke the It ScriptBlock (Again)**

    – Executes the second test within the new isolated scope.

    – Validates the outcome based on the Should statement.

7. **Return to Previous Scope (Again)**

    – Reverts to the outer scope after completing the second test.

8. **Repeat Until All Tests Complete**

   – Continues this pattern for each test in the script.

9. **Return to Outermost Scope**

   – Concludes the Run Phase.

Common Gotchas

The Run Phase introduces some potential pitfalls that are essential to navigate:

1. **BeforeAll** and **-ForEach**

   – **-ForEach** is evaluated during Discovery, but **BeforeAll** won't run until the Run Phase.

   – Using variables set in BeforeAll in -ForEach won't work since the variable won't be defined until after -ForEach is evaluated. For example, the following code in Listing 6-3 will not work as expected.

Listing 6-3. Ignoring Pester rules results in unexpected outcomes

```
BeforeAll {
    $result = 5
}
Describe "Unexpected Results" {
    It "Adds numbers" -ForEach @(
        @{ Action = "Add one"; Expected = ⮑ ($result + 1)}
        @{ Action = "Add two"; Expected = ⮑ ($result +2)}
    ) {
        #Invoke-Wonder -Action $Action | Should ⮑
        - Be $Expected
        write-host "running test Five $action = ⮑ $expected"
    }
}
```

Running this test would result in the output shown in Figure 6-1.

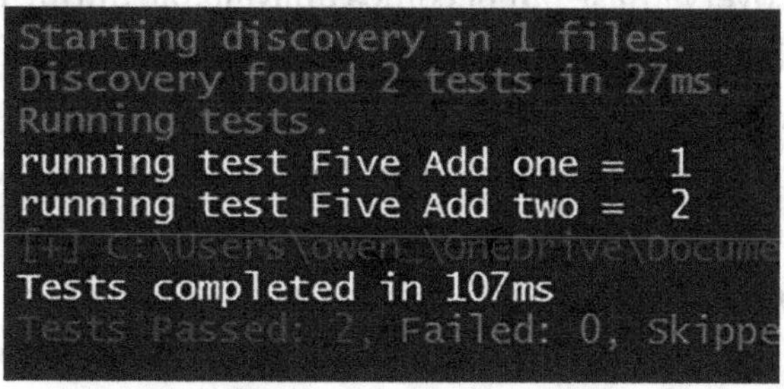

Figure 6-1. *Unexpected results*

That's definitely not the desired outcome. To fix this, replace the **BeforeAll** block with **BeforeDiscovery**, and you're good to go.

2. **Generating Tests via ForEach Keyword**

   – If using -ForEach to generate tests based on external data, ensure that the code generating tests is defined in the BeforeDiscovery block. We saw an example of this in Listing 6-2 earlier.

Note   An Exploration of Pester Behavior

The official Pester documentation provides an illustrative example:

```
$name = "Jakub"

Describe "d" {
    It "My name is: $name" {
        $name | Should -be "Jakub"
    }
}
```

The documentation clarifies that executing this test will result in failure. According to the explanation, the **$name** variable is evaluated during the Discovery Phase but becomes unavailable during the Run Phase. Interestingly, in my experience, the test passed, possibly indicating a version-specific behavior or bug in my Pester version.

However, it's crucial to adhere to best practices. Even if the test currently passes, defining variables outside of appropriate script blocks may lead to unexpected behavior in different Pester versions. To ensure consistent and reliable test outcomes, it's recommended to follow best practices and confine variable definitions within the designated script blocks. This approach aligns with the principles of robust testing and minimizes the risk of potential issues in diverse Pester environments.

Navigating the Run Phase

Let's continue delving into the Run Phase with the insightful example provided in Listing 6-4. We're equipped with the illustrative function **Invoke-Wonder** and two data-driven tests.

Listing 6-4. Exploring the Run Phase

```
function Invoke-Wonder {
    param (
        [string]$Action
    )

    # Perform some marvelous action based on the input
    # For the sake of this example, let's simplify it
    switch ($Action) {
        "Sparkle" { 'Success' }
        "Thunder" { 'Powerful' }
        default { 'Unknown' }
    }
```

```powershell
}

BeforeAll {
    # Set up your environment or import necessary modules
}

Describe "PowerShell Wonders" {
    It "Performs Marvelous Feats" -ForEach @(
        @{ Action = "Sparkle"; Expected = 'Success'}
        @{ Action = "Thunder"; Expected = 'Powerful'}
    ) {
        Invoke-Wonder -Action $Action | Should -Be $Expected

        Write-host "Run phase complete"
    }
}
Write-Host "Discovery phase complete"
```

Here's what happens:

1. The script file is invoked, triggering the Run Phase.

2. The **BeforeAll** script block executes to prepare the testing environment before any tests are run.

3. The **Describe** block encapsulates our tests, specifically the **It** block, which performs the "marvelous feats" using the **Invoke-Wonder** function.

4. For each data-driven test specified in the **-ForEach** loop, the **It** block runs, invoking **Invoke-Wonder** with the provided parameters and validating the outcome using **Should -Be**.

5. The **Write-Host** "Run phase complete" statement confirms the completion of the Run Phase for each iteration of the data-driven test.

The output of running these tests is shown in Figure 6-2.

```
Starting discovery in 1 files.
Discovery phase complete
Discovery found 2 tests in 19ms.
Running tests.

Running tests from 'C:\ohtemp4\runphase.tests.ps1'
Describing PowerShell Wonders
Run phase complete
      [+] Performs Marvelous Feats 14ms (6ms|7ms)
Run phase complete
      [+] Performs Marvelous Feats 6ms (4ms|1ms)
Tests completed in 115ms
Tests Passed: 2, Failed: 0, Skipped: 0 NotRun: 0
```

Figure 6-2. Run Phase output

Now you have a solid understanding of the Run Phase, you gain insight into the sequential execution of your script, enabling you to navigate the intricacies of test scenarios and ensure a robust and predictable testing environment.

Visualizing the Phases: Discovery and Run

We have explored the intricacies of Pester's Discovery and Run Phases now, so let's visualize their interplay through a concise table and a simple yet meaningful code sample.

The table in Figure 6-3 provides a quick reference to the execution behavior of script blocks in both the Discovery and Run Phases.

Phase	V5 Discovery	V5 Run
BeforeAll	✗	✓
BeforeEach	✗	✓
It	✗	✓
AfterEach	✗	✓
AfterAll	✗	✓
BeforeDiscovery	✓	✗
Describe	✓	✗
Context	✓	✗
Other	✓	✗

Figure 6-3. *Execution of script blocks in Pester phases*

Note   "Other" represents anything outside of the **BeforeAll**, **BeforeEach, AfterEach, AfterAll**, and **It** blocks.

Script Showcase: The Choreography of Discovery and Run

Let's illustrate the seamless transition from Discovery to Run with a meaningful code sample. In Listing 6-5, we use **Write-Host** to clearly show the path taken during both the Discovery and Run Phases of our fictitious test suite evaluating an imaginary authentication function.

Listing 6-5. The trajectory followed by the Discovery and
Run Phases

```
Write-Host "Commencing the journey of discovery."

BeforeDiscovery {
    Write-Host "Tasks unfold during discovery."
}

Describe "User Authentication Tests" {
    Write-Host "Setting the stage for user authentication ⮎
    tests."

    It "Validates user login" {
        Write-Host "Test1: I am in the run phase"
        Write-Host "Executing user login validation."
        # Actual test logic goes here
    }

    It "Verifies user access rights" {
        Write-Host "Test2: I am in the run phase"
        Write-Host "Executing user access rights ⮎
        verification."
        # Actual test logic goes here
    }

    Write-Host "Completed setup for user authentication ⮎
    tests."
}

Write-Host "Discovery phase concludes. Preparing for the run."
```

If you were to run this test (and you can, should you wish), then the
following output shown by Figure 6-4 is presented on screen.

```
Starting discovery in 1 files.
Commencing the journey of discovery.
Tasks unfold during discovery.
Setting the stage for user authentication tests.
Completed setup for user authentication tests.
Discovery phase concludes. Preparing for the run.
Discovery found 2 tests in 1.17s.
Running tests.
Test1: I am in the run phase
Executing user login validation.
Test2: I am in the run phase
Executing user access rights verification.
[+] C:\ohtemp4\test2.ps1 5.46s (840ms|3.63s)
Tests completed in 5.63s
Tests Passed: 2, Failed: 0, Skipped: 0 NotRun: 0
```

Figure 6-4. *Note that any code in the **Write-Host** statements outside of the allowed script blocks comes under "Other" and are executed during Discovery*

As I embarked on my journey to master Pester, I encountered the frustration of seemingly inexplicable test failures. It didn't take long to realize that my struggles were rooted in a lack of understanding of Pester's phases. With the insights gained from this chapter, I aim to pass on those hard-earned lessons, ensuring that any future missteps in your Pester coding journey will be uniquely yours!

Summary

In this chapter, we embarked on a comprehensive exploration of the fundamental phases that define the Pester testing framework: Discovery and Run. Much like a skilled director plans each scene in a play, understanding these Pester phases is crucial for orchestrating effective tests. The chapter delved into the intricacies of the Discovery Phase, where Pester identifies and prepares the stage for testing, and the Run Phase, where the actual performance unfolds.

The Discovery Phase, the bedrock for Pester 5 features, was thoroughly examined. The significance of adhering to certain practices during this phase was highlighted, emphasizing best practices in test code placement. An illustrative example showcased the impact of misplaced code during Discovery, underlining the importance of following recommended practices. The introduction of BeforeDiscovery marked a pivotal point in intentional code placement outside controlled blocks, with a unique example illustrating its role in dynamic test generation.

Transitioning to the Run Phase, the chapter highlighted its role in executing tests and unraveled the execution order complexity introduced in Pester version 5. Common pitfalls, such as the evaluation timing of BeforeAll and -ForEach, were explored, reinforcing the importance of BeforeDiscovery. Pester behavior exploration discussed an illustrative example from official documentation, emphasizing the need to adhere to best practices for consistent and reliable test outcomes.

A practical example using Invoke-Wonder and data-driven tests was provided to showcase the sequential flow of tests during the Run Phase. The importance of understanding the Run Phase was underscored for creating robust and predictable testing environments.

The interplay between Discovery and Run Phases was visualized through a concise table, providing a quick reference to the behavior of script blocks in both phases.

A meaningful code sample in Listing 6-4 illustrated the seamless transition from Discovery to Run using Write-Host to clearly show the path taken during both phases of a fictitious test suite evaluating an imaginary authentication function.

As we conclude this chapter, armed with a solid understanding of Discovery and Run Phases, you are well prepared to navigate the complexities of Pester testing. In Chapter 7, we'll delve into TestDrive and TestRegistry, empowering you with tools to take your Pester expertise to the next level.

CHAPTER 7

TestDrive and TestRegistry

In this chapter you will discover two invaluable tools – TestDrive and TestRegistry. They'll transform your testing practices from a free-for-all into a carefully orchestrated symphony.

TestDrive, your personal testing sandbox, provides a safe haven to test your scripts without fear of collateral damage. Think of it as a magical playground where you can create temporary files, modify them freely, and test interactions at will, only to have everything vanish neatly afterward, leaving your actual file system pristine.

TestRegistry, on the other hand, offers a temporary, isolated space within the Windows registry for your tests to interact with. Imagine it as a virtual registry sandbox, allowing you to safely test registry-related functions without worrying about unintended changes to your real system.

So fire up your ISE of choice and let's take your testing game to the next level!

TestDrive

Have you ever dreamed of a testing playground where you can unleash your scripts with reckless abandon, knowing your real system remains untouched? (And no, I don't mean your production environment!) Well, say hello to TestDrive! This powerful tool creates a temporary, isolated

© Owen Heaume 2024
O. Heaume, *Getting Started with Pester 5*, https://doi.org/10.1007/979-8-8688-0306-2_7

environment where you can create, modify, and delete files at will, all vanishing like smoke when your test concludes. Imagine it as a sandbox for all of your file testing needs, where you can experiment freely without fear of breaking the real-world file system.

Behind the TestDrive Curtain

TestDrive might appear like a magical land for file-based testing, but it's actually powered by a clever trick under the hood. Instead of a separate physical drive, it utilizes a temporary directory within your system, creating a controlled and isolated environment for your tests. Here's how it works:

1. **Creating the temporary space:** When you activate TestDrive, PowerShell generates a unique folder nestled within your temporary (%temp%) directory (`C:\Users\<username>\AppData\Local\Temp\<guid>`). This folder acts as the root of your TestDrive "drive," housing any directories and files you create within it.

2. **Weaving the drive illusion:** PowerShell creates a symbolic link in your system's "drive space," connecting it to the hidden temporary folder. This link makes the temporary folder appear as a separate drive called **TestDrive:**. Now, when you interact with files and directories within TestDrive, you're actually manipulating files inside this special <guid> folder.

3. **Maintaining the sandbox:** TestDrive ensures your test actions are isolated from your real system. Files created within TestDrive won't affect your existing files or folders as it is dynamically created. As an added bonus, the temporary folder and its contents are automatically removed after each test run, leaving no trace of your testing.

There are multiple benefits to this approach:

- **Isolation:** Each test has its own dedicated sandbox, preventing accidental modifications to your real system and ensuring consistent testing conditions.

- **Efficiency:** No physical drive creation or removal is involved, making TestDrive lightweight and efficient.

- **Transparency:** While the internal mechanism is unique, you interact with TestDrive as a regular drive, simplifying test code and keeping things easy to use.

Setting Up Your TestDrive Playground

Ready to create your temporary file haven? Here's how you do it:

Inside a Pester test block: Ensure you're within a **Describe** or **Context** block in your Pester test script. (TestDrive is designed to work within these testing structures.)

Activate the TestDrive by using the command:

```
New-Item -Path TestDrive:\YourDirName -ItemType Directory
```

This creates a new temporary drive named **TestDrive:**, ready for your file experiments.

The code snippet in Listing 7-1 illustrates this.

Listing 7-1. Creating TestDrive

```
Describe "Using TestDrive" {
    BeforeEach {
        New-Item -Path TestDrive:\myDir -ItemType Directory
    }

    It "Creates a temporary file" {
        # Your file creation code here
    }
}
```

Playing with Files in Your Sandbox

Now that your TestDrive is open for business, let's play with some files!

Creating files: Use standard PowerShell commands like New-Item or Out-File to create files within the TestDrive: directory.

Modifying files: Edit file contents using commands like Set-Content, Add-Content, or even good old text editors.

Reading files: Use Get-Content or other file reading techniques to access file data within TestDrive.

Deleting files: Employ Remove-Item to delete files from the sandbox.

Listing 7-2 is an example demonstrating file creation and reading.

Listing 7-2. Creating a file in TestDrive and reading its contents

```
Describe "Using TestDrive" {
    BeforeEach {
        New-Item -Path TestDrive:\file.txt -ItemType File ↳
```

```
# Create the file
    }

    It "Creates a temporary file and writes content" {
        Set-Content -Path TestDrive:\file.txt -Value ↳
        "Hello, TestDrive!"

        $fileContent = Get-Content -Path TestDrive:\file.txt
        ↳  # Use full path
        $fileContent | Should -Be "Hello, TestDrive!"

    }
}
```

If we navigate to the temporary location of our TestDrive (C:\
Users\<username>\AppData\Local\Temp\<guid>) as shown in Figure 7-1,
we can see the directory named after a random guid and the created file.
Once the test has finished running, the whole thing is removed, and it was
like it was never there in the first place.

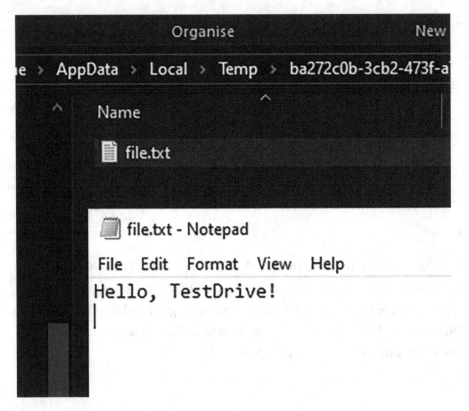

Figure 7-1. *The magic of TestDrive!*

Creating Directories and Files in the Sandbox

While TestDrive automatically sets up a temporary drive, explicitly creating directories within it is crucial for organization and reliability. Here's how you do it:

```
New-Item -Path TestDrive:\myDir -ItemType Directory -Force
```

The -Force parameter ensures directory creation even if a folder with the same name already exists, preventing potential conflicts.

Use the **BeforeEach** block to set up the TestDrive environment before each test, guaranteeing a clean slate and consistent conditions. This includes creating both directories and files as shown in Listing 7-3.

Listing 7-3. Creating both a directory and a file

```
BeforeEach {
    New-Item -Path TestDrive:\myDir -ItemType Directory -Force
    New-Item -Path TestDrive:\myDir\file.txt -ItemType File ⤷
    # Create the file
}
```

Treat TestDrive as a separate drive within your tests, using paths like *TestDrive:\myDir\file.txt* to work with files and directories within it. This is demonstrated in the test shown in Listing 7-4.

Listing 7-4. Referencing files within TestDrive

```
Describe "Using TestDrive" {
    BeforeEach {
        # Explicitly create the TestDrive directory
        New-Item -Path TestDrive:\myDir -ItemType Directory ⤷
        -Force
        New-Item -Path TestDrive:\myDir\file.txt ⤷
        -ItemType File  # Create the file
    }

    It "Creates a temporary file and writes content" {
        Set-Content -Path TestDrive:\myDir\file.txt ⤷
        -Value "Hello, TestDrive!"

        $fileContent = Get-Content -Path ⤷ TestDrive:\myDir\
        file.txt
        $fileContent | Should -Be "Hello, TestDrive!"
    }
}
```

Keeping It Simple

For simplicity and flexibility, you may wish to assign a variable to the file path used by TestDrive. In Listing 7-5, we assign the **$path** variable and reuse it in the code for clarity.

Listing 7-5. Using a variable to reference the path

```
Describe "Using TestDrive" {
    BeforeEach {
        # Explicitly create the TestDrive directory
        New-Item -Path TestDrive:\myDir -ItemType ↵
        Directory -Force
        $path = New-Item -Path TestDrive:\myDir\file.txt ↵
        -ItemType File  # Create the file
    }

    It "Writes content to a temporary file" {
        Set-Content -Path $path -Value "Hello, TestDrive!"

        $fileContent = Get-Content -Path $path
        $fileContent | Should -Be "Hello, TestDrive!"
    }
}
```

Using a variable with TestDrive is considered a good practice for several reasons:

Readability and Maintainability

- **Explicit path storage:** Using **$path** to store the file path makes the code more readable and easier to understand.

- **Centralized path management:** You can update the path in one place if needed, rather than changing multiple occurrences throughout the code.

- **Reduced redundancy:** It eliminates the need to repeat the same path string multiple times, making the code cleaner and less prone to errors.

Flexibility and Reuse

- **Variable manipulation:** You can manipulate the path variable using string operations if needed, such as constructing dynamic paths for different scenarios.

- **Reuse in multiple tests:** The same path variable can be easily reused across different tests that work with the same file or directory, promoting consistency and reducing code duplication.

Consistency

- **Enforced path usage:** Using a variable ensures that the same path is always used consistently throughout the test code, reducing the risk of errors due to typos or inconsistencies.

You can see now how the standard PowerShell best practices can also be applied to your Pester code. Don't lose sight that at the end of the day, it's all just PowerShell.

Cleaning Up with a Snap

Once your test concludes, TestDrive automatically vanishes, taking all its temporary files with it – it's like a magical self-cleaning kitchen! However, for super-robust tests, consider the following:

1. **Error checking:** Add **try-catch** blocks to handle potential TestDrive creation failures.

2. **Manual cleanup:** Implement an **AfterEach** block with `Remove-Item -Path TestDrive:\ myDir -Recurse -Force -ErrorAction SilentlyContinue` to remove any leftover files, especially when dealing with concurrent tests, external processes, or file permissions.

Let's dive into Listing 7-6 to witness how PowerShell accommodates these robust testing practices.

Listing 7-6. Creating robust tests with error checks and cleanups

```
Describe "Using TestDrive" {
    BeforeEach {
        try {
            # Explicitly create the TestDrive directory
            New-Item -Path TestDrive:\myDir -ItemType ↵
            Directory -Force -ErrorAction stop
            New-Item -Path TestDrive:\myDir\file.txt ↵
            -ItemType File -ErrorAction Stop # Create the file
        } catch {
            Write-Error "Failed to create TestDrive ↵
            directory or file: $($_.Exception.Message)"
            throw
        }
    }

    AfterEach {
        Remove-Item -Path TestDrive:\myDir -Recurse ↵
        -Force -ErrorAction SilentlyContinue
    }

    It "Creates a temporary file and writes content" {
        Set-Content -Path TestDrive:\myDir\file.txt ↵
        -Value "Hello, TestDrive!"

        $fileContent = Get-Content -Path ↵ TestDrive:\myDir\
        file.txt
        $fileContent | Should -Be "Hello, TestDrive!"
    }
}
```

Let's decipher Listing 7-6, line by line, to reveal TestDrive's magic in action!

Scene 1: Setting the Stage (BeforeEach)

- **"try { ... } catch { ... }":** This vigilant duo guards against unexpected mishaps during setup.

- **New-Item -Path TestDrive:\myDir -ItemType Directory -Force:** With a wave of its wand, TestDrive conjures a temporary directory named "myDir" within its realm. The -Force ensures no obstacles stand in its way.

- **New-Item -Path TestDrive:\myDir\file.txt -ItemType File:** A blank text file, aptly named "file.txt", materializes within "myDir", ready to serve as a testing canvas.

Scene 2: Cleaning Up the Act (AfterEach)

- **Remove-Item -Path TestDrive:\myDir -Recurse -Force -ErrorAction SilentlyContinue:** Like a diligent stagehand, this command sweeps away all traces of "myDir" and its contents, restoring TestDrive to its pristine state. No lingering props or forgotten lines here!

Scene 3: The Main Performance (It)

- **Set-Content -Path TestDrive:\myDir\file.txt -Value "Hello, TestDrive!":** The script takes center stage, scribing the message "Hello, TestDrive!" onto the blank canvas of "file.txt".

- **$fileContent = Get-Content -Path TestDrive:\myDir\file.txt:** Like an attentive audience member, this line absorbs the contents of "file.txt", storing them within the "$fileContent" variable.

– **$fileContent | Should -Be "Hello, TestDrive!":** The grand finale! A critical assertion verifies that the message written to the file matches the expected text, ensuring a flawless performance.

And thus, the curtain falls on a successful test, leaving TestDrive's stage empty and ready for the next act!

Key Points to Remember

– TestDrive is scoped to the test block where it's created. Files in one block won't be visible in another.

– Explicitly create subdirectories within TestDrive.

– TestDrive works seamlessly with relative paths for easy file navigation.

– Perform error checking and manual cleanup for even greater confidence in your tests.

With these insights, you're now fully equipped to conquer TestDrive! Let's move on to its sibling: TestRegistry next.

TestRegistry

TestDrive may have swept you off your feet with its temporary file haven but prepare to be further enraptured by TestRegistry! This magnificent tool grants you a secluded space within the Windows registry, a virtual playground where your tests can interact with registry keys and values without a trace on your actual system. It's like a sandbox, cloaked from the prying eyes of your real registry, ensuring uninhibited testing without fear of unintended modifications.

Behind the TestRegistry Curtain

Similar to TestDrive, TestRegistry operates under a clever disguise. While it appears to interact directly with the registry, it actually constructs a temporary key within the registry's HKEY_CURRENT_USER\Software\Pester\<RandomGUID> location.

This key serves as the foundation for your virtual registry sandbox, mirroring the structure of your real registry for seamless interaction during testing.

Let's Craft Your Virtual Registry Sandbox

To create your own isolated TestRegistry sandbox, include the following line within either an **It**, **BeforeEach**, or **BeforeAll** block of your Pester test script:

```
New-Item -Path "TestRegistry:\" -Name MyTestKey
```

This command lays the groundwork for your virtual registry sandbox, ready to accommodate your testing endeavors.

Interacting with Your Virtual Realm: A Practical Demonstration

Now that your TestRegistry is ready, let's try it out! Listing 7-7 shows how you can create a registry key and set a value within your virtual sandbox.

Listing 7-7. Creating a registry key and value using TestRegistry

```
Describe "Using TestRegistry" {
  BeforeEach {
    New-Item -Path "TestRegistry:\" -Name MyTestKey
  }
}
```

```
It "Creates a registry key and sets a value" {
    New-ItemProperty -Path "TestRegistry:\MyTestKey" ↵
    -Name 'MyValue' -Value "Hello, TestRegistry!"

    $value = Get-ItemProperty -Path ↵
    "TestRegistry:\MyTestKey" -Name 'MyValue' | select ↵
    -ExpandProperty 'myvalue'
    $value | Should -Be "Hello, TestRegistry!"
  }
}
```

Figure 7-2 shows TestRegistry in action. Once the tests have finished, it's all cleaned up.

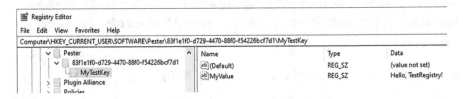

Figure 7-2. *TestRegistry creates a random GUID key while testing. It's deleted when the tests have completed*

Listing 7-7 Under Scrutiny

In this example

1. Create a test block named "Using TestRegistry."

2. Ensure a clean test key before each test using **BeforeEach**.

3. The New-ItemProperty command creates the MyValue value within the MyTestKey key of the TestRegistry hive.

4. The Get-ItemProperty command retrieves the value of MyValue, and the Select-Object -ExpandProperty 'MyValue' part extracts the actual value from the resulting object.

5. The retrieved value is then compared to the expected text using the Should assertion.

Remember   TestRegistry is a powerful tool for safe registry testing. Always use TestRegistry for registry-related tests.

Like a self-cleaning oven, TestRegistry automatically vanishes once your test concludes, taking all its created keys and values with it.

Cleaning Up with a Snap

While TestRegistry typically cleans up after itself, incorporating robust error handling and manual cleanup is wise for exceptional reliability. Here's how you can add an **AfterEach** block for extra reassurance:

```
AfterEach {
    Remove-Item -Path "TestRegistry:\" -Recurse -Force ↵
    -ErrorAction SilentlyContinue
}
```

This command ensures that any leftover traces of your TestRegistry activities are removed, leaving your virtual sandbox spotless for the next test encounter.

Key Points to Remember

- Each test block receives its own isolated TestRegistry hive, ensuring pristine conditions for every test.

- You can create, modify, and delete registry keys and values within the TestRegistry hive just like you would in the real registry.

- Once your test concludes, the entire TestRegistry hive vanishes, leaving no trace of your testing adventures within the real registry.

With TestRegistry as your ally, you can confidently venture into registry testing, knowing that your actual system remains safe and sound. It doesn't get much better than that!

Summary

In this chapter, we discovered TestDrive and TestRegistry, unlocking their powers to elevate your Pester testing practices.

TestDrive emerged as your personal testing haven, a temporary file system where you can unleash your scripts without fear of repercussions. You learned how to create, modify, and delete files within this secluded sandbox, ensuring your actual system remains pristine. We explored the BeforeEach and AfterEach blocks, mastering the art of setting up and cleaning up your testing environment.

Next, we ventured into the hidden depths of the registry with **TestRegistry**. This magnificent tool granted you a virtual registry sandbox, a playground for interacting with keys and values without jeopardizing your real system's stability, empowering you to tailor your virtual registry environment to match your testing needs.

With TestDrive and TestRegistry as your allies, you're now equipped to tackle even the most intricate testing scenarios with confidence. No longer are you confined by the boundaries of your real system; you can freely explore, experiment, and gain valuable insights, all while safeguarding the delicate balance of your core environment.

As we turn the page to Chapter 8, prepare to delve into the captivating world of **Tags and Invoke-Pester**.

CHAPTER 8

Tags and Invoke-Pester

Your Pester test suite is growing and, with it, the complexity of managing its execution. Running every test every time becomes impractical, hindering agility and efficiency.

This chapter introduces two powerful tools, **tags** and **Invoke-Pester**, that transform your test suite into a finely tuned instrument for targeted and controlled execution.

Imagine this: Categorize your tests with intuitive tags, then effortlessly run only the tests relevant to your current needs. No more wading through irrelevant scripts or wasting time on unnecessary runs. Invoke-Pester acts as your conductor, seamlessly orchestrating the execution of specific tagged groups, freeing you from manual effort and empowering streamlined testing workflows.

Beyond basic runs, this chapter opens up a world of possibilities for optimized testing strategies. Learn how to

- Design efficient testing scenarios focused on specific areas or functionalities.
- Reduce overall test run time by eliminating irrelevant tests.

Dreaming of a test suite that's organized, flexible, and efficient? This chapter holds the key to unlocking an efficient testing experience.

© Owen Heaume 2024
O. Heaume, *Getting Started with Pester 5*, https://doi.org/10.1007/979-8-8688-0306-2_8

Tag Along! Organizing Your Pester Tests with Tags

Imagine your test suite as a bustling library – shelves upon shelves filled with books (tests) covering various topics. Finding the specific book (test) you need amid this vast collection can be overwhelming. Thankfully, just like libraries categorize their books with genres and labels, Pester offers tags to organize and manage your tests effectively.

What Are Tags?

Think of tags as simple keywords or labels that you can assign to your tests. Imagine them as sticky notes categorizing your test's purpose, functionality, or target area.

These tags become powerful filters, allowing you to

Group-related tests: Have tests for different modules in your application? Tag them with the corresponding module name, allowing you to run just the tests relevant to that specific module. For example, you could tag tests for user authentication with "UserLogin" and module-specific functionality with "ModuleA".

Focus on specific functionalities: Need to verify a particular feature? Add a "feature_X" tag to relevant tests and run them independently. This allows you to focus your testing efforts on specific areas of concern.

Identify and exclude outdated tests: Mark deprecated tests with a "deprecated" tag and easily filter them out during execution. This keeps your test suite clean and organized, ensuring you're testing relevant functionalities.

Why Use Tags?

Whether you're a beginner or an experienced tester, using tags offers significant benefits:

Reduced complexity: Organize your tests with tags improves clarity and make your test suite easier to understand and navigate. This is especially helpful as your test suite grows more complex.

Focused testing: Run only the tests relevant to your current needs, saving you time and resources. Imagine being able to quickly test a newly added feature without running the entire suite!

Efficient debugging: Quickly identify and isolate failing tests based on their tags. This helps you pinpoint the root cause of issues much faster.

Enhanced collaboration: Shared tagging conventions improve communication and understanding within testing teams. Everyone involved can easily understand what each test covers and why it's tagged the way it is.

Adding Tags to Your Tests

Adding tags is simple! You can assign them to your **Describe**, **Context,** and **It** blocks, similar to labeling different sections of a book as demonstrated in Listing 8-1.

Listing 8-1. Tag! You're it!

```
# Tagging a Describe block
Describe "Module A Tests" -Tag 'ModuleA' {
  # Tests for Module A here
}

# Tagging a Context block
Context "Feature X Functionality" -Tag 'FeatureX' {
  # Tests for Feature X here
}

# Tagging an It block
It "Checks user login functionality" -Tag 'UserLogin' {
  # Test for user login here
}
```

Now, imagine you only need to verify *FeatureX* functionality. Using Invoke-Pester with the -TagFilter parameter, you can specifically run just the tests tagged with "FeatureX":

```
Invoke-Pester -Path .\mytestfile.tests.ps1 -TagFilter
'FeatureX'
```

This command executes only the tests within the Context block tagged with "FeatureX," saving you time and effort.

Case-Insensitivity and Multi-tagging: Supercharging Your Test Organization

Tags in Pester offer powerful flexibility, not only in grouping functionalities but also in how you use them. Let's delve into two key advantages.

Case-Insensitivity: Freedom from Typo Worries

Imagine accidentally typing "usercreation" instead of "UserCreation" for a tag. Don't fret! Pester treats tags as case-insensitive. Whether you write "usErCrEaTiOn" or "USERCREATION," Pester recognizes them all as the same tag, ensuring your tests remain easily discoverable and executable regardless of capitalization variations. This flexibility saves you from headaches and wasted time due to minor typos.

Multi-tagging: Granular Organization at Your Fingertips

Tags aren't limited to one-dimensional categorization. You can leverage multiple tags separated by a comma (`-Tag 'Tag1', 'Tag2'`), to create a more fine-grained organization within your test suite.

This empowers you to

Combine broad and specific tags: Tag a test with "UserManagement" for its general category and "ResetPassword" for its specific functionality.

Combine platform-specific tags: Test functionality on different platforms. Add tags like "Windows" or "Linux" alongside your core functionality tags.

Refine test selection: By using multiple tags, you can construct precise filters for test execution. Need to run all tests related to user management on Linux? Simply use `Invoke-Pester -Path .\mytestfile.tests.ps1 -TagFilter 'UserManagement', 'Linux'`.

Tagging in Action: Unleashing Efficiency

Let's venture into a practical example, applying tags to organize your user management tests:

- **UserCreation:** Tag relevant tests with "UserCreation," further categorized by "Success" and "Validation" to differentiate between successful scenarios, validations, and preventing invalid user creation attempts. This granular organization provides clear insights into different aspects of user creation.

- **RoleAssignment:** Employ tags like "RoleAssignment" and "DefaultRole" to categorize tests for assigning default or custom roles. This makes it easy to understand and test each role assignment scenario.

- **PasswordReset:** Tag tests with "PasswordReset" and "Complexity" to group those verifying password reset functionality and password complexity enforcement. This helps ensure robust password security measures are in place.

- **ProfileUpdate:** Include tags like "ProfileUpdate" and "ContactInformation" to identify tests verifying profile updates and specific data changes. This targeted approach allows you to focus on specific user profile functionalities.

Listing 8-2 showcases tagged tests.

Listing 8-2. A tagging example

```
Describe "User Creation Tests" -Tag 'UserCreation' {
    Context "Successful User Creation" -Tag 'Success' {
        It "Should create a user with valid inputs" ↵
```

```
-Tag 'Validation' {
            # Test logic for successful user creation
        }
    }

    Context "Invalid User Creation Attempts" ↵
    -Tag 'Invalid' {
        It "Should prevent duplicate usernames" ↵
        -Tag 'Validation' {
            # Test logic for preventing duplicate usernames
        }

        It "Should reject invalid email formats" {
            # Test logic for validating email format
        }
    }
}

Describe "Role Assignment Tests" -Tag 'RoleAssignment' {
    It "Should assign new users to the default role" {
        # Test logic for default role assignment
    }

    It "Should allow assigning custom roles to users" {
        # Test logic for custom role assignment
    }
}

Describe "Password Reset Tests" -Tag 'PasswordReset' {
    It "Should allow password reset via email" {
        # Test logic for password reset via email
    }

    It "Should enforce password complexity rules" ↵
```

```
        -Tag 'Complexity' {
        # Test logic for password complexity enforcement
    }
}

Describe "Profile Update Tests" -Tag 'ProfileUpdate' {
    It "Should allow updating contact information" ↩
    -Tag 'ContactInformation' {
        # Test logic for updating contact information
    }

    It "Should prevent unauthorized profile changes" {
        # Test logic for security measures in profile updates
    }
}
```

Excluding Tests: The Magic of -Skip and Tags

We've explored the power of tags to categorize and organize your Pester tests. But what if you want to temporarily silence certain tests or groups? Enter the -Skip parameter and its tag-based companion, offering you precise control over test execution.

Excluding with -Skip

The -Skip parameter lets you temporarily disable whole **Describe** or **Context** blocks or individual tests:

```
It "Test for feature X (currently disabled)" -Skip {
  # Test code here
}
```

Note   It's important to use this feature responsibly and avoid skipping large portions of your test suite for extended periods. However, the ability to skip Describe and Context blocks can be helpful for temporarily disabling noncritical tests or excluding tests that are incompatible with specific environments.

Now when you run your test suite with Invoke-Pester, anything with -skip will be skipped as demonstrated in Listing 8-3.

Listing 8-3. Demonstrating skipping tests with the -Skip tag in Invoke-Pester

```
Describe "Tagged Tests" {
    it "will not be skipped" {
        $true | should -BeTrue
    }

    it "will be skipped" -Skip {
        $true | should -BeTrue
    }

    it "will also not be skipped" {
        $true | should -BeTrue
    }
}
```

And the resulting output shown in Figure 8-1 clearly shows tests were skipped.

115

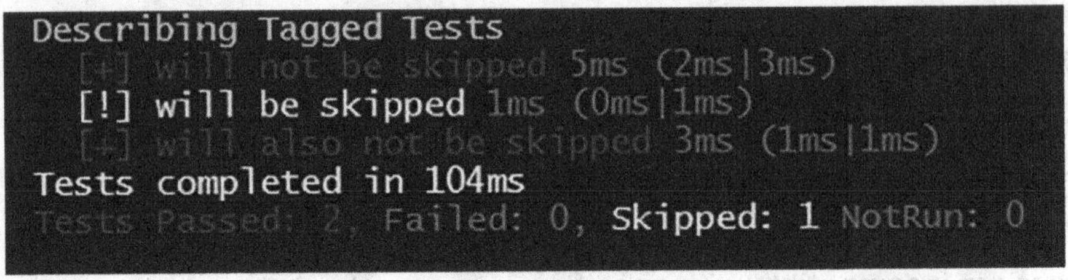

Figure 8-1. *Skipped tests are still displayed in the output*

While simple, this approach can become cumbersome for excluding multiple tests.

Leveraging Tags for Exclusion

Here's where tags shine! Create a "skip" tag and assign it to tests you want to exclude:

```
It "Test for feature Y (skipped)" -Tag 'Skip' {
  # Test code here
}
```

Now, you can use Invoke-Pester with the -ExcludeTag parameter to exclude all tests with the "Skip" tag:

```
Invoke-Pester -Path .\mytestfile.tests.ps1 -ExcludeTag 'Skip'
```

This effectively excludes all tests marked with "Skip," while other tagged or untagged tests run normally.

Advanced Exclusion Strategies

Combining -Skip and -ExcludeTag: Combine both for granular control. Exclude entire tagged groups while still skipping specific tests within other groups.

Dynamic exclusion: Use variables or external data sources to determine exclusion criteria based on your testing needs. (Although this is beyond the scope of this beginner's book.)

Remember   Excluded tests are skipped, not hidden. Their existence is still reported, allowing you to track them for future inclusion.

By mastering exclusion techniques, you can

- Temporarily disable unstable or in-progress tests without affecting others.

- Focus testing efforts on specific areas while excluding irrelevant or outdated tests.

- Simplify large-scale test suites by keeping them organized and manageable.

Start employing tags and exclusion strategies to transform your Pester test suite into a well-oiled testing machine, ensuring focused, efficient, and controlled testing practices!

Unleash Granular Testing Power: Running Specific Test Types with Ease

Imagine yourself standing before a vast testing landscape, eager to delve into specific areas. Perhaps you yearn to scrutinize the intricate interactions between components (integration tests) or carefully examine individual units in isolation (unit tests). While manually executing each test might be feasible for a small test suite, it quickly becomes cumbersome and inefficient as your tests multiply.

Let's see how Pester can help us to tackle these problems.

Running Specific Tests with Ease: Your Guide to Pester Efficiency

Let's face it, testing every single test every time can be like searching for a specific snowflake in a blizzard! Especially when your test suite grows, targeting only the tests you need becomes crucial. Thankfully, Pester has some tricks up its sleeve to help you focus your testing efforts.

Naming Your Tests for Clarity

Imagine your test files as labeled boxes in a storage unit. To quickly find the boxes you need, clear labels are key. This is where naming conventions come in!

Add a prefix: Use a prefix before **.tests.ps1** with a word that tells you what kind of tests they are. For example, use "integration.tests.ps1" for tests that check how different parts of your code work together and "unit. tests.ps1" for tests that examine individual pieces of code in isolation. For instance, MyFunction.**unit**.tests.ps1 or MyFunction.**integration**. tests.ps1

Keep it descriptive: Don't just write "**test1**.tests.ps1" – give each test a meaningful name that explains what it does. This will make it much easier to understand what you're testing, even if you haven't seen the code in a while.

Finding Tests with "Invoke-Pester"

Now that your tests are clearly labeled, let's unleash the power of **Invoke-Pester** to pinpoint the exact tests you need!

Wildcards for File-Based Filtering

Zero in on specific file types: Imagine you want to run all integration tests. Simply use `Invoke-Pester -Path "*integration.tests.ps1"`. The asterisk (*) acts as a wildcard, matching any test file name that begins with "integration.tests".

Tags for Cross-file Execution

Organize tests beyond file boundaries: Assign common tags to related tests, even if they reside in different .tests.ps1 files. This grants you the flexibility to group and execute tests based on their purpose, not location.

Targeted execution across files: Use `Invoke-Pester` with the `-Tag` parameter to execute tests bearing a specific tag, regardless of their file. For example, `Invoke-Pester -Tag "Integration" -Path *.tests.ps1` runs all "Integration" tagged tests found within **any** .tests.ps1 file in the current directory.

Key Points

Both wildcards and tags provide distinct ways to filter and execute tests effectively.

Wildcards focus on file names, while tags offer a more functional grouping approach that transcends file boundaries. Choose the method that best suits your testing needs and preferences.

Benefits of Targeted Testing

Running specific tests has some awesome advantages:

> **Faster testing:** No more waiting for hundreds of tests to run when you only need a few. This saves you valuable time and resources.

119

Sharper focus: By targeting specific types of tests, you can concentrate on pinpointing issues in specific areas. This makes debugging and understanding problems much easier.

Organization matters: A well-structured test suite with clear naming and tagging is easier to navigate and maintain, especially as it grows.

By using these techniques, you can transform your Pester testing from a blizzard of tests to a focused and efficient process, ensuring your code is rock-solid!

Summary

This chapter has equipped you with the power to navigate your Pester test suite with ease and efficiency. We explored the magic of tags, transforming them from simple labels into powerful tools for organizing, filtering, and running specific tests. You've also learned:

Excluding with finesse: Temporarily silence specific tests or groups with `-Skip` and `-ExcludeTag`, keeping your suite organized.

The art of naming: Clear and descriptive test file names and individual test labels make your suite intuitive and easy to navigate.

Wielding wildcards: Target entire categories of tests based on file names using wildcards like `*integration.tests.ps1`

Tagging for power: Group related tests across different files using tags, enabling focused execution based on functionality, not location.

Harnessing these techniques doesn't just save you time and resources: it transforms your entire testing approach. Instead of waiting for hundreds of tests to run, you can zoom in on specific areas of concern, executing only the tests that matter most. This sharpens your focus, allowing you to debug issues with greater ease.

But the benefits extend beyond immediate execution. Clear naming, tagging, and exclusion strategies foster a well-organized and manageable test suite. As your suite grows, this structure becomes invaluable, ensuring clarity and maintainability.

Ultimately, targeted testing isn't just about efficiency; it's about building a rock-solid foundation for confident code. By using the tools outlined in this chapter, you empower yourself to write better code, identify problems faster, and deliver a higher-quality product, one focused test at a time.

Now that you've mastered targeted execution, let's delve deeper into the world of mocking. Imagine isolating specific parts of your code and manipulating their behavior for testing purposes. This is the magic of mocking covered in the next chapter. I'll forewarn you now, it's a long chapter, so ensure you are well rested and hydrated, and get ready to learn how to elevate your testing to a whole new level!

## CHAPTER 9

Mocking Your Way to Success

When I first ventured into the world of Pester and stumbled upon the concept of mocking, I have to admit, it left me scratching my head. It was one of those things that I knew existed, but I couldn't quite grasp why or when I should use it. It felt like I was missing a crucial piece of the puzzle.

But fear not! In the chapter ahead, we're going to take a deep dive into the world of mocking. I won't sugarcoat it; this is going to be a bit of a marathon chapter. However, by the time we're through, you'll know not only what mocking is but also why it's an essential tool in your testing toolkit. So, let's roll up our sleeves and get ready to demystify mocking together.

What Is Mocking?

Mocking is like creating a mimic of a function or cmdlet. When you employ mocking in your Pester test, let's say for the sake of illustration, you're dealing with something like `Test-Path`, essentially, you're telling your test that when your function runs and would typically call upon `Test-Path`, substitute it with the mock instead. In other words, it prevents the actual execution of the real `Test-Path` cmdlet when you call the function from within your Pester test.

O. Heaume, *Getting Started with Pester 5*, https://doi.org/10.1007/979-8-8688-0306-2_9

In unit tests, the goal is to avoid touching any real services or file systems. It's crucial to maintain a controlled and predictable testing environment. Think of it as having a stand-in actor take the stage while the real star takes a break – all part of making your tests more controlled and precise.

Why Use Mocks to Avoid Real Services?

Mocking is like having a double for a superstar, but its significance extends beyond just improving the accuracy of your tests. In a world where software interacts with various services, databases, or external systems, using mocks becomes paramount for several reasons.

Let's consider a scenario where your code interacts with an external service, like a file system. In a typical testing environment, making actual calls to these services could lead to several challenges:

1. **Test environment independence:** Real services can introduce dependencies that make your tests environment specific. Your tests may work perfectly on one machine but fail on another due to differences in the environment.

2. **Data consistency:** When you touch the file system or interact with external services, you may alter data unintentionally. This can lead to unpredictable test outcomes and potentially destructive side effects.

3. **Speed and efficiency:** Real services can be slow or unreliable. Waiting for file system operations or external service responses can significantly slow down your tests, making them inefficient and less productive.

This is where mocks come to the rescue. When you substitute a real service call with a mock, you gain control and predictability over your tests.

Imagine your code is expected to fetch data from a remote API. Instead of making actual requests to that API, you create a mock that simulates the API's behavior. You instruct the mock to return specific responses under various conditions.

For instance, you can configure the mock to return mock data when your code requests it. This allows you to simulate different scenarios, such as successful responses, timeouts, or error conditions, without ever making a real network request, allowing your code to be tested for each scenario.

By using mocks, you ensure that your tests remain independent of external factors, maintain data consistency, execute swiftly, and consistently deliver reliable results. It's like having a rehearsal for a high-stakes performance – you control the script, and the show goes on flawlessly, no matter the complexities of the real world.

Continuing the previous example of mocking `Test-Path`, in your function, you might be dynamically sending a path to be tested and executing different code depending on whether the path exists or not. Now, let's think about why using mocks, in this case, is incredibly valuable.

Imagine you have a function that's responsible for processing files. Before it takes any action on a file, it needs to determine if the file exists using `Test-Path`. Based on whether the file is there or not, your function makes decisions like whether to process it, skip it, or perform some other action, and it is these decisions that we are interested in testing.

Now, during testing, you don't want your Pester tests to actually touch the file system. That's where the power of mocking shines. By substituting `Test-Path` with a mock, you gain control over the testing environment. You can instruct the mock to behave as if the file exists or doesn't exist, simulating various scenarios without altering the real file system. Remember, we are interested in testing the branching conditions of our code which take place depending on the output of `Test-Path` without conducting a "real" `Test-Path` call to a real file system.

For instance, if you're testing how your function handles a missing file scenario, you can set up the mock to always return "false" for Test-Path. This ensures that your function's logic for handling missing files is thoroughly tested, without the need for actual files to be present or deleted during testing. The pester test calls your function, and your function executes Test-Path (the mock, not the real thing) which has been configured to output "false," and now you can test if the function logic handles the false response correctly.

On the flip side, when you're testing the case when the file does exist, you can configure the mock to return "true" for Test-Path, allowing you to verify that your function behaves correctly in that situation.

So, in essence, mocks in your Pester tests act as directors on a film set, guiding the actors (functions and cmdlets) and scripting the scenes (testing scenarios) to ensure that your code performs flawlessly under various conditions, all while keeping the real world safely at bay.

Let's consolidate this with some example code. Listing 9-1 shows an example function: **Invoke-FileOperation**.

Listing 9-1. Invoke-FileOperation

```
function Invoke-FileOperation {
    param (
        [string] $filePath
    )

    # Check if the file exists using Test-Path
    if (Test-Path -Path $filePath) {

        # File exists, perform processing
        Write-Host "Processing file: $filePath"

        # Additional processing logic here

        return $true
```

```
} else {
    # File does not exist, handle accordingly
    Write-Host "File not found: $filePath"

    # Additional handling for missing files

    return $false
  }
}
```

In this example, the **Invoke-FileOperation** function takes a $filePath parameter and performs a file operation. It uses Test-Path to check whether the specified file exists in the file system. Based on the result of this check, the function makes decisions:

- If the file exists (Test-Path returns **$true**), it outputs a message indicating that it's processing the file and may perform additional processing logic. Finally, it returns true to indicate a successful operation.

- If the file doesn't exist (Test-Path returns **$false**), it outputs a message stating that the file was not found and may include additional handling for missing files. It returns false to indicate that the operation encountered an issue due to the file's absence.

This function serves as an example of how real services, like file system interactions, can be incorporated into your code. However, it also illustrates the need for mocking when testing, as you don't want your tests to depend on the actual file system's state. Mocking Test-Path in your tests allows you to simulate different file existence scenarios and thoroughly test how your code handles them. With that said, I'm going to throw you into the deep end now. Listing 9-2 shows what Pester tests might look like for this function.

Listing 9-2. Our Pester tests for the Invoke-FileOperation function

```
BeforeAll {
    . $PSCommandPath.Replace('.tests',"")
    Mock Write-Host
}

Describe "Invoke-FileOperation function" {
    Context "When the file exists" {
        It "Should process the file" {
            Mock Test-Path { return $true }

            $result = Invoke-FileOperation -filePath ↳
            "C:\sample.txt"
            $result | Should -BeTrue
        }
    }

    Context "When the file does not exist" {
        It "Should handle the missing file" {
            Mock Test-Path { return $false }

            $result = Invoke-FileOperation -filePath ↳
            "C:\nonexistent.txt"
            $result | Should -BeFalse
        }
    }
}
```

In this example shown in Listing 9-2, we have a Pester test script designed to validate the behavior of the **Invoke-FileOperation** function we discussed earlier. Let's break down the various sections.

BeforeAll Block

```
BeforeAll {
    . $PSCommandPath.Replace('.tests',"")
    Mock Write-Host
}
```

The **BeforeAll** block sets up some initial conditions for the tests. It includes two key actions:

1. **$PSCommandPath.Replace('.tests',"")**: We've covered this earlier in the book so I'll just jog your memory: this line dot sources the main PowerShell script that contains the function by replacing ".tests" in the script's path with an empty string. This step ensures that the main script is loaded into memory and available for testing.

2. **Mock Write-Host**: Here, we are mocking the Write-Host cmdlet. In Pester tests, it's a common practice to mock cmdlets that produce output to prevent unnecessary console output during testing.

Note   In this case, the Write-Host cmdlet is not mocked with any specific behavior or replacement action. Instead, it's set up to be "quiet" by returning nothing. When Write-Host is called within the function being tested, the mock will take over, but it essentially does nothing.

Why Mocking Write-Host Matters: The significance of this mock lies in its silence. By using this mock, you ensure that when the Write-Host cmdlet is called within your function, it doesn't produce any actual output during testing. This helps maintain a clean and focused testing environment.

What Happens If You Don't Mock Write-Host: If you were to comment out this line and not mock `Write-Host`, the actual `Write-Host` cmdlet would be invoked when your tests run. As a result, you would see the `Write-Host` output on your screen, which can clutter your testing results and make it more challenging to isolate the actual test outcomes from extraneous console messages. (Figure 9-1 shows the extraneous messages that were not suppressed, cluttering the test results.)

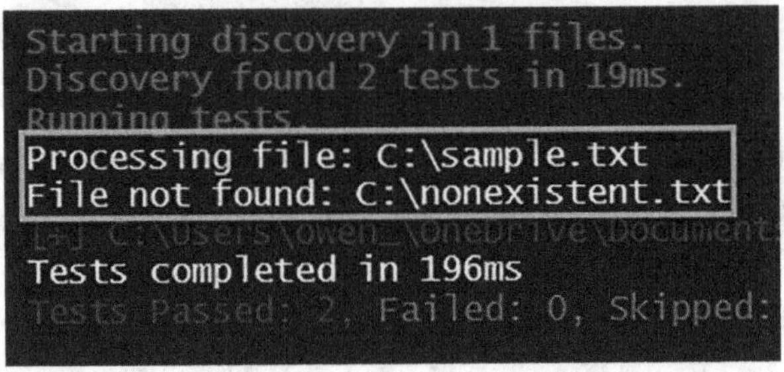

Figure 9-1. *Unwanted "noise" can make it difficult to read test results*

So, by including this mock without specific replacement actions, you ensure that `Write-Host` stays silent during testing, keeping your test results clear and focused on the behavior of your function.

Describe Block

```
Describe "Invoke-FileOperation function" {
    ...
}
```

The **Describe** block provides a logical grouping for your tests and serves as a descriptive label for what you're testing. In this case, it describes the testing of the "Invoke-FileOperation" function.

Context Blocks

```
Context "When the file exists" {
    ...
}
Context "When the file does not exist" {
    ...
}
```

Within the **Describe** block, we have two **Context** blocks. Each Context represents a different scenario that we want to test:

- The first context, "When the file exists," simulates a scenario where the specified file exists.

- The second context, "When the file does not exist," simulates a scenario where the specified file is missing.

So far so good? It's all ground we've already covered in previous chapters. Now on to the good part.

IT Block

```
It "Should process the file" {
    ...
}
It "Should handle the missing file" {
    ...
}
```

Inside each **Context** block, we have **It** blocks. Each **It** block represents a specific test case or assertion. They specify what the expected behavior should be for the given scenario.

In the first **It** block, we test that when the file exists, the function should process it. We use the **Mock** cmdlet to control the behavior of Test-Path, and we expect the result to be **True** using Should -BeTrue.

In the second **It** block, we test that when the file does not exist, the function should handle the missing file. Again, we use the **Mock** cmdlet to simulate Test-Path, and we expect the result to be **False** using Should -BeFalse.

So we have effectively tested our code logic by simulating different file existence scenarios, ensuring that our **Invoke-FileOperation** function behaves as expected under both file existence and nonexistence conditions.

These Pester tests ensure that your **Invoke-FileOperation** function behaves correctly under different file existence scenarios, all without actually touching the real file system.

A Little More Between the Curly Braces, Please

When using **Mock**, the portion between the curly braces { and } defines what the mock will return. As you observed in the earlier example Mock Test-Path { Return $true }, when Test-Path is called and replaced by the mock, it returns $true. Your code, in turn, interprets this result as if Test-Path genuinely returned $true, and it proceeds based on that response.

However, you can also use the curly braces to return nothing, effectively silencing the command being mocked. This is similar to what we did when we mocked Write-Host. Leaving out any content between the curly brackets, like in Mock-Write-Host { }, achieves the same result – the mocked command is silenced, and it doesn't produce any output or return any values.

So, the content between the curly braces defines what the mock returns, and you can use this to control the behavior of the mocked command, whether it's returning specific values or producing silence during testing.

Mocking Best Practices

The golden rule of mocking: Mimic reality, but don't go overboard. Think of it as imitating a chef's recipe; you want the taste to be authentic, but you don't need to replicate the entire kitchen.

In our previous example of mocking `Test-Path`, how did I know to mock the return as **true** or **false**? I simply looked at PowerShell's `Help Test-Path` and unearthed this gem: *"The 'Test-Path' cmdlet determines whether all elements of the path exist. It returns '$True' if all elements exist and '$False' if any are missing."*

You can also dump the return in a variable and inspect its contents to see the type of data being returned, use `GetType()` or pipe to `Get-Member` if you need to find out the object type. I usually end up with my mocks returning a hashtable in most cases though, and you'll see this shortly.

Now, here's the trick: while you aim to mirror the real command, you don't need to mimic every nook and cranny. Imagine you're crafting a sculpture; you chisel away only what's necessary to reveal the masterpiece within. `Test-Path` was easy; it returns a Boolean, and that's it but take something like `Get-ADUser`, for instance; it spills out a treasure trove of properties, but maybe you need only a handful, so simply return the ones you need.

So, as we journey forward, keep this balance in mind. Our mocks should echo reality but be tailored to suit our specific needs.

Here's a handy list I put together of some mocking best practices that I try to follow and that you should also consider when creating your mocks:

1. **Mimic real behavior:** Mock commands as close to their real behavior as possible. Understand the real command's outputs and behaviors by referring to official documentation or help files. By replicating real-world responses, your tests reflect actual application scenarios more accurately.

2. **Keep it simple:** While it's essential to mimic real behavior, don't overcomplicate mocks. Focus on the specific behavior your code interacts with. Complex mocks can make tests convoluted and harder to maintain.

3. **Be consistent:** Maintain consistency in your mocks. If you mock a command in one test scenario, use similar patterns in other relevant scenarios. Consistency enhances the readability and comprehension of your test suite.

4. **Update mocks with code changes:** When your actual code changes, ensure that corresponding mocks are updated. Mismatched mocks can lead to inaccurate tests, providing a false sense of security.

5. **Avoid tight coupling:** Mock only what your code directly interacts with. Avoid overly tight coupling where a change in the underlying implementation forces extensive changes in your tests. Mocking should shield your tests from implementation details.

6. **Documentation is your friend:** Rely on official documentation, help files, and specifications when determining how to mock specific commands. Understanding the intended behavior helps create accurate mocks.

Beware of Pitfall #5 in the preceding list – steering clear of tight coupling. In my initial foray into the realm of mocking, I meticulously mocked every detail, down to the precise messages emitted by Write-Host. (You'll see how later.) However, when I subsequently altered the message text within my functions, chaos ensued. All my tests came crashing down like a house of cards.

By adhering to these best practices, your tests become powerful tools for ensuring your code's correctness, resilience, and maintainability. Now that you have a strong foundation, let's continue this lengthy chapter, building on the principles you've learned so far.

Mocking Complex Cmdlets

By now, you've mastered the art of mocking straightforward commands like Test-Path. You've gained the confidence to manipulate their behaviors, crafting your tests with finesse. But what about the more complex cmdlets, the likes of get-aduser, Invoke-RestMethod, or Import-Csv? These multifaceted tools don't merely return true or false; they churn out intricate data structures, arrays, and hashtables.

Fear not, for the Mock cmdlet is still your trusty companion on this journey. It possesses incredible depth beyond the binary world of true and false. Within those curly braces, you can conjure a universe of possibilities – a PSCustomObject, an Array, a Hashtable, or even an array of hashtables, and the list goes on.

Once I had personally figured this part out, my mocking prowess evolved from Billy-Basic to Henry-Hero. Suddenly, there was nothing in the PowerShell realm that I couldn't mock, no complexity too great to simulate.

Stay with me, and I'll guide you through this transformation. Together, we'll unravel the secrets of mocking these intricate cmdlets, empowering you to wield PowerShell's mightiest tools with finesse. After perusal of the next few pages, you will be stepping confidently into the realm of Henry-Hero mocking.

PSCustomObject

Imagine you have a function called **Get-ServerInfo**. Its job? Reading data from a CSV file and doing something with it. Simple, right? Well, reality often throws curveballs – the CSV file you're expecting might not be there on the computer running your tests.

But here's the catch: we don't really care about the CSV file itself; as just alluded, the test may be run on a system that does not have access to the real CSV. We just want to know what our function does with the data. And here's where PSCustomObject becomes your buddy.

PSCustomObject can help you pretend that your function imported data from a CSV file, even if it didn't really. It's like giving your function imaginary data to play with. How? Well, you create a pretend data set like this:

```
$MockedData = @(
    [PSCustomObject]@{
        Property1 = 'Value1'
        Property2 = 'Value2'
        # ...add more properties if needed
    }
)

Mock Import-Csv { return $MockedData }
```

With this trick, your function can keep chugging along, imagining it's working with real data. PSCustomObject ensures your tests stay smooth and predictable, even when the real world throws a few surprises your way.

It's worth noting that I've enclosed the entire [PSCustomObject] and its properties in brackets so that it becomes an array of PSCustomObjects: @([PSCustomObject]...). This setup allows you to create more than one "row" in your simulated CSV by adding additional PSCustomObjects. Essentially, it becomes an array of PSCustomObjects. If your needs are simpler and you only require one custom object, you can omit the brackets entirely. Flexibility is the key here – tailor your approach to match the complexity of your data simulation needs.

Let me show you what I mean with an example:

```
function Get-ServerInfo {

    $servers = Import-Csv -Path 'C:\OHTemp\Servers.csv'

    return $servers.count
}
```

The function reads in a CSV file and returns the number of servers found in the CSV file. Not very practical in the real world but good enough to hammer home the concept here. Listing 9-3 demonstrates how a test could look for it.

Listing 9-3. Testing the Get-ServerInfo function

```
Describe 'Get-ServerInfo' {
    Context 'When given a valid CSV file' {
        It 'Returns the correct number of servers' {
            #Arrange
```

```
            $MockedData = @(
                [PSCustomObject]@{
                    Name = 'Server1'
                    OS   = 'Windows Server 2019 Standard'
                };
                [PSCustomObject]@{
                    Name = 'Server2'
                    OS   = 'Windows Server 2012 R2'
                }
            )

            mock Import-Csv { $MockedData }

            #Act
            $expected = Get-ServerInfo

            #Assert
            $expected | Should -Be 2
        }
    }
}
```

Remember, when the test calls the function **Get-ServerInfo** and `Import-CSV` is executed, it swaps it out for your mocked `Import-Csv` and mocked data. The real `Import-Csv` is never called within your function. Clever stuff!

There's More Than One Way to Skin a Cat

Now, let's explore an alternative approach when dealing with CSV files, revealing the versatility of Pester and encouraging you to think "outside the box" when crafting your tests.

Consider this: what if we achieve the same test results using ConvertFrom-CSV and a here-string to simulate the CSV data? Let's take a peek at how this scenario unfolds in the script snippet in Listing 9-4.

Listing 9-4. An alternative method

```
Describe 'Get-ServerInfo' {
    Context 'When given a valid CSV file' {
        It 'Returns the correct number of servers' {
            #Arrange
            mock import-csv {
                ConvertFrom-Csv -InputObject @'
'Name','OS',
'Server1','Windows Server 2019 Standard'
'Server2','Windows Server 2012 R2'
'@
            }

            #Act
            $expected = Get-ServerInfo

            #Assert
            $expected | Should -Be 2
        }
    }
}
```

This alternative method not only showcases the power of Pester but also prompts you to consider innovative solutions when shaping your test cases.

Hashtables

When it comes to my mocking adventures, I often find myself relying on hashtables. Much like with PSCustomObjects, I encapsulate them in an array by wrapping them in brackets: @().

Let's dive into an example, shown in Listing 9-5, where we mock Get-Module using an array to simulate the return of multiple versions of the same installed PowerShell module.

Listing 9-5. Mocking Get-Module

```
Describe 'My Pester test' {
    It 'does something wonderful' {
        #Arrange
        Mock Get-Module {
            @{ Version = '1.0.9'; Name = 'MyModule'}
            @{ Version = '1.0.5'; Name = 'MyModule'}
            @{ Version = '1.0.2'; Name = 'MyModule'}
        }

        # Act...

        # Assert...
    }
}
```

In this scenario, the use of hashtables within an array enables us to brilliantly mimic the behavior of Get-Module, returning various versions of the same module.

It's all about crafting your mocks to mirror the real-world scenarios, ensuring your tests are as robust as your imagination allows.

When to Use a PSCustomObject over a Hashtable

Knowing when to opt for a PSCustomObject over a hashtable is pivotal in PowerShell scripting. As a personal preference, I usually resort to arrays of hashtables. They're simple to create, easy on the eyes, and universally comprehensible. However, there are situations that call for the elegance of a PSCustomObject.

If a cmdlet produces a PSCustomObject as its output, I follow suit. Consistency is key; if the cmdlet provides data in this format, it makes sense to mirror it. Furthermore, if your scripting ventures lead you to the realm of strongly typed properties – where a property must be explicitly defined as a certain data type (like string or int) – PSCustomObject emerges as the hero.

Consider this scenario: you need to define properties like this.

```
[PSCustomObject]@{
    Name = [string]"John"    # Name property is ↵
    explicitly defined as a string
    Age = [int]30            # Age property is ↵
    explicitly defined as an integer
}
```

Or you may need to return a specific type of object and for that PSCustomObject wins again with its PSTypeName Declaration:

```
[PSCustomObject]@{
    PSTypeName = WhateverObjectTypeYouNeed
    Name = 'MyName'
}
```

In such cases, PSCustomObject becomes your trusted companion. Its ability to accommodate well-defined data types ensures precision in your scripts.

Import-CliXML

The `Import-CliXML` cmdlet presents a powerful mocking technique, especially for scenarios involving API calls. Whenever I saw Pester examples using API calls I always thought they were bad examples as I had never needed to use them. One career change later and whammo! Suddenly, a wave of PowerShell API tasks flooded my workspace, proving that you never quite know what challenges lie ahead. So it would therefore be remiss if we did not include API mocks in our examples too.

Traditionally, mocking API calls involved intricate maneuvers. However, a straightforward method emerged: calling the API for real and capturing its response in an XML file. This captured "snapshot" could then fuel our mocks, ready for testing. Allow me to illustrate.

Consider a function shown in Listing 9-6.

Listing 9-6. Example function using an API call

```
function Get-ThingToDo {
    $result = Invoke-RestMethod -Method Get -Uri ↵
    "https://www.boredapi.com/api/activity"

    if ($result.type -eq "Relaxation") {
        return $true
    } else {
        return $false
    }
}
```

In this function, the real API response is captured in the **$result** variable. If the 'Type' property is "Relaxation," it returns True; otherwise, it returns False. To mock this response, ensuring precise outcomes *without* real API calls, we employ Import-CliXML.

Firstly, we need to capture a real response. To capture the API response, simply pipe Invoke-RestMethod to Export-Clixml, as demonstrated in Listing 9-7.

Listing 9-7. Capturing the real API response for later use

```
Invoke-RestMethod -Method Get -Uri ↳
"https://www.boredapi.com/api/activity" | ↳
Export-Clixml C:\OHTemp\Response.xml
```

This command generates an XML file at the specified location, ready for use in our mock. In Listing 9-8, we integrate this captured response into our test.

Listing 9-8. Integrating the captured API response into the mock

```
Describe "Get-ThingToDo" {
    it "Should return True if Type is 'Social'" {

        Mock Invoke-RestMethod {
            Import-Clixml "C:\ohtemp\Response.xml"
        }

        $Expected = Get-ThingToDo

        $Expected | should -BeTrue
    }
}
```

In this way, we harness the real-world API response to create mocks, ensuring accurate and reliable tests. It's a testament to the adaptability of PowerShell and Pester, empowering us to handle unexpected challenges with finesse.

.Net Classes

Now, let's delve into the scary world of .Net classes to demonstrate the flexibility of mocks. Consider a scenario where you're working with Invoke-WebRequest and want to specifically catch errors generated by [System.Net.WebException] within a try-catch block. The function, defined in Listing 9-9, looks like this.

Listing 9-9. The Get-Error function to be tested

```
Function Get-Error {
    try {
        $response = Invoke-WebRequest -Uri "https://
        fearthepanda.com/notexist" -Method
        get -ErrorAction stop
    } catch [system.net.webexception] {
        write-host "The error was $_"
        return 1
    }
}
```

In this function, the catch block targets errors of type [System.Net. WebException] and returns 1. The corresponding Pester test, found in Listing 9-10, ensures this behavior is as expected.

Listing 9-10. Testing error handling

```
Describe "Get-error" {
    it "Should return 1" {
        $webException = New-MockObject -Type System.Net.
        WebException

        Mock Invoke-WebRequest {
            throw $webException
        }

        Mock write-host

        $Expected = Get-Error

        $Expected | should -Be 1
    }
}
```

Within the **It** block, the Mock command simulates the Invoke-WebRequest call. It uses New-MockObject to create a **System.Net. WebException** object with the default error message and then throws the [System.Net.WebException] to replicate the real scenario of Invoke-WebRequest encountering an error. This mock ensures the **Get-Error** function handles [System.Net.WebException] as anticipated, returning 1.

In general, you would employ New-MockObject to create a mock object based on the .Net Type, a topic that falls outside the scope of this book. While diving deeper into mocking .Net classes can get intricate and complex, this glimpse should pique your curiosity, encouraging you to explore this topic further and gain a deeper understanding.

But Wait, There's More!

So, .Net can be a bit of a maze, right? But fear not, you don't have to get lost in it. There are tricks to navigate these complexities, and I'm here to share a couple of them with you.

1. **Embrace Native PowerShell:** Why complicate things with .Net when PowerShell itself can often do the job? Take the example of retrieving the environment variable windir. Sure, you could use the .Net approach:

   ```
   [Environment]::GetEnvironmentVariable('windir')
   ```

   But then you're setting yourself up for a headache when it's time to mock it in your tests. Instead, opt for the native PowerShell equivalent:

   ```
   Get-Item -Path 'env:windir'
   ```

   Simple, elegant, and best of all, easily mockable in your tests. No more wrestling with .Net intricacies.

2. **Wrapping .Net Commands in PowerShell Functions: A Mocking Strategy:** Now, what if you can't find a native PowerShell alternative? Don't worry, there's a workaround. Wrap the .Net command in a cozy PowerShell function. Let's say for some reason you just *have* to fetch an environment variable using .net. Simply wrap it in a function as shown in Listing 9-11.

Listing 9-11. Encapsulating a .net command within a function

```
Function Get-EnvironmentVariable {
    [cmdletbinding()]

    param (
        [string]$Variable
    )

    $envVar = [Environment]::GetEnvironmentVariable($Variable)

    if (-not ($envVar)) {
        Write-Host "$Variable not found"
        return 1
    } else {
        return $envvar
    }
}
```

In this concise function, the intricate .Net call is encapsulated, providing a clear interface. This not only enhances readability but also renders mocking a seamless endeavor during testing.

Let's illustrate this concept further with an example. Imagine you have a function, as demonstrated by Listing 9-12.

Listing 9-12. Sample function

```
Function My-AmazingFunction {
    param (
        [string]$EnvVar
    )

    if ($EnvVar) {
        $result = [Environment]::GetEnvironmentVariable
        ($Variable)
```

```
        return $result
    } else {
        Write-Output "You didn't want to get the environment
        variable"
        return $false
    }
}
```

In the initial script, Listing 9-12, we encounter a common problem: direct invocation of a .Net command within the function. Specifically, the line:

```
$result = ⮡ [Environment]::GetEnvironmentVariable($Variable)
```

While this approach may seem straightforward, it poses a significant challenge during testing. When attempting to unit test this function, a crucial problem emerges: the .Net method `[Environment]::GetEnvironment Variable($Variable)` directly interacts with the operating system, fetching environment variables in real time. In the realm of testing, unpredictability becomes the enemy. We can't guarantee the existence or values of these variables in different environments.

This unpredictability creates a testing nightmare. How do we write reliable tests when the function's behavior depends on external, ever-changing factors? Enter the need for a solution: Listing 9-13.

Listing 9-13. Refactor the function to easily test .Net

```
Function My-AmazingFunction {
    param (
        [string]$EnvVar
    )

    $result = Get-EnvironmentVariable -Variable $EnvVar
```

```
if ($result -ne 1) {
    $result
} else {
    Write-Host "You didn't want to get the ↳
    environment variable"
    return $false
}
}
```

Understanding the Transformation: From Listing 9-12 to Listing 9-13

In Listing 9-12, the script undergoes a crucial transformation. (We already alluded to earlier in the book that Pester likes you to refactor your functions!) The direct invocation of the .Net method is replaced with a function call:

```
$result = Get-EnvironmentVariable -Variable $EnvVar
```

Here, Get-EnvironmentVariable acts as a protective shield. It encapsulates the unpredictable .Net operation within a controlled environment. By wrapping the .Net call in a PowerShell function (see Listing 9-11), we achieve two critical goals:

1. **Predictability for testing:** The function can now be mocked during tests. Instead of unpredictably interacting with the OS, the function can return predefined values, making tests reliable and consistent.

2. **Readability and maintainability:** The script becomes more readable. The intention behind fetching the environment variable is encapsulated in a function with a clear name (Get-EnvironmentVariable), enhancing the script's readability and making maintenance easier.

This transformation not only resolves testing challenges but also contributes to the script's overall robustness and maintainability. By understanding and addressing the inherent issues via Listing 9-11, we pave the way for more predictable, manageable, and reliable PowerShell scripting.

To test the functionality now, we can craft Pester tests like Listing 9-14.

Listing 9-14. Testing the refactored function

```
Describe My-AmazingFunction {

    it "Should return the variable if it exists" {
        # Arrange
        mock Get-EnvironmentVariable { "SampleValue"}

        # Act
        $expected = My-AmazingFunction -EnvVar "SampleValue"

        # Assert
        $expected | should -be "SampleValue"
    }

    it "Should return the False if the variable does ⤸
    not exist" {
        # Arrange
        mock Get-EnvironmentVariable { }

        # Act
```

```
    $expected = My-AmazingFunction -EnvVar "SampleValue"

    # Assert
    $expected | should -beFalse
  }
}
```

Listing 9-14 Explained

In the first **It** block, the mock Get-EnvironmentVariable { "SampleValue" }
statement is setting up a mock for the Get-EnvironmentVariable function.

This mock is simulating the behavior of the real Get-
EnvironmentVariable function and returning the string "SampleValue".

When My-AmazingFunction -EnvVar "SampleValue" is called, it uses
the mocked Get-EnvironmentVariable function, which always returns
"SampleValue". The Assert section then checks if the returned value
matches the expected value "SampleValue".

In the second **It** block, the mock Get-EnvironmentVariable { }
statement sets up a mock for the Get-EnvironmentVariable function that
returns nothing, simulating the behavior when the environment variable
does not exist.

When My-AmazingFunction -EnvVar "SampleValue" is called, it
also uses the mocked Get-EnvironmentVariable function, which now
returns nothing. The Assert section then checks if the returned value is
False, indicating that the function correctly handles the scenario when the
environment variable does not exist.

With these strategies up your sleeve, you'll be taming .Net intricacies
like a pro.

Verifying Your Mocks: Ensuring Your Logic Is Sound

So, you've mastered the art of mocking. Your functions are beautifully crafted, your tests are comprehensive, and everything seems to be working as expected. But how can you be absolutely certain that your mocks are doing what they're supposed to do? This is where verification steps in.

Consider this scenario: you've set up a mock for Test-Path. You know it should be called when your function runs, but how can you prove it? Verification allows you to confirm that your logic is sound and that your function is interacting with the mock as intended.

Take, for instance, this sample function in Listing 9-15, **Get-Path**.

Listing 9-15. The sample Get-Path function

```
function Get-Path {
    param (
        [parameter (Mandatory = $true,ValueFromPipeline ↳
        = $true)]
        [string]$Path
    )

    process {
        if (test-path $path) {
            write-host "The path exists"
            return $true
        } else {
            write-host "The path does not exist"
            return $false
        }
    }
}
```

It takes a path, checks its validity, and writes a message accordingly. Now, if you send a path like "C:\I\Exist", you'd expect Test-Path to be called once. Similarly, if you send two paths down the pipeline, it should be called twice.

The Pester test script for validating this function could be structured as demonstrated in Listing 9-16, which shows tests that validate *Test-Path* was called the correct number of times.

Listing 9-16. Testing the Get-Path function

```
Describe "Get-Path" {
    BeforeAll {
        Mock Write-Host
    }

    Context "When sending a path" {
        It "Returns True if the path is valid" {
            # Arrange
            $path = "C:\I\Exist"
            Mock test-path {$true}

            # Act
            $expected = Test-Path -Path $path

            # Assert
            $expected | Should -BeTrue
            Should -invoke Test-path -times 1 -Exactly
        }

        It "Returns False if the path is not valid" {
            # Arrange
            $path = "C:\I\Do\Not\Exist"
            Mock test-path {$false}
```

```
        # Act
        $expected = Test-Path -Path $path

        # Assert
        $expected | Should -BeFalse
        Should -invoke Test-path -times 1 -Exactly
    }
}

context "when sending via the pipeline" {
    It "should call the mock the correct number↩
    of times" {
        # Arrange
        Mock test-path {$true}

        # Act
        "c:\Exists", "c:\AlsoExists" | Get-Path

        # Assert
        Should -Invoke Test-path -times 2 -Exactly
    }
}
}
```

This concept comes to life in your Pester tests. In Listing 9-16 you create different contexts to test your function's behavior. When testing a direct path, you assert that **Test-Path** is called once and only once:

```
should -invoke Test-path -times 1 -Exactly
```

In the pipeline context, where two paths are sent, ("c:\path1","c:\ path2" | Get-Path), you adjust the **-times** parameter accordingly:

```
should -invoke Test-path -times 2 -Exactly
```

Here's the key: using `-times 2 -Exactly` ensures that **Test-Path** is called precisely twice. This level of verification gives you confidence that your function is interacting with the mock exactly as planned. Without using `-exactly,` the test would pass if **Test-Path** was called *at least* two times.

Tip   You also have the option to employ `-Times 0` if you want to ensure with absolute certainty that a command is not called at all or, alternatively, use the `-not` parameter to achieve the same result: `Should` **`-not`** `-Invoke Test-path`

By verifying your mocks in this way, you're not just writing tests; you're ensuring the integrity of your functions. It's a crucial step that adds a robust layer of reliability to your PowerShell scripts.

Understanding the Verification Line

Let's wrap this section up by taking a little more time to make sure the verification line is fully understood before we continue the next part of our mocking journey.

This is the line that performs the verification magic:

```
should -invoke Test-Path -times 1 -Exactly
```

Here's how it works:

- **Should:** We've covered this earlier in the book: This keyword is fundamental in Pester. It's like your testing assistant, allowing you to set expectations about what your code should do. It's your way of saying, "Hey, PowerShell, I expect this to happen."

- **Invoke test-path:** Here, you're specifying the command or function that you're keeping an eye on. In our case, it's Test-Path. You want to ensure that this specific command is executed.

- **Times 1:** This part indicates how many times you expect your command to be called. In the code snippet provided earlier, `Test-Path` should be invoked once. Think of it like counting instances. If your function loops and calls `Test-Path` multiple times, this number should match the total count.

- **Exactly:** This parameter is key. It emphasizes precision. You're not just saying "I want it to be called at least once." (which is what would happen if you omitted this parameter), but you're stating, "I want it to be called exactly once, no more, no less." It ensures the command is behaving as you've planned.

Imagine you're baking cookies. You want to make sure the oven timer rings exactly once when your cookies are done. If it rings too early, your cookies might be undercooked. If it rings too late, they could burn. Setting `-times 1 -Exactly` is akin to ensuring that precise timing, guaranteeing your cookies (or in this case, your function) turn out just right.

Using a Parameter Filter

In this section, we explore the powerful feature of `-ParameterFilter` within Pester's Mock command, a tool designed to ensure your mocks are invoked with precise parameter values. This parameter serves as a gatekeeper, allowing the mocked behavior only if the incoming parameters meet the criteria defined in the filter. It's crucial to note that if the filter conditions are not met, the original command will be invoked instead of the mock, potentially leading to unexpected behavior.

Why Would You Use -ParameterFilter?

This feature shines when you need to test diverse code paths in your functions. Imagine a scenario where a function behaves differently based on the input parameters. With -ParameterFilter, you can precisely mock the command and its varied outputs, allowing you to thoroughly test different code paths.

How to Use -ParameterFilter

To leverage this filter, you simply define which parameters you want to ensure are passed, encapsulating them within a script block. If you have more than one parameter to consider, you can employ PowerShell's comparison operators like **-eq**. For instance, let's take **Get-Item** as an example. It has a -Path property. To guarantee that the mock is invoked only when a specific path is used, you can employ the -ParameterFilter like this:

```
Mock Get-Item {} -ParameterFilter { $Path -eq "C:\MyPath" }
```

This construct allows you to precisely control when your mock executes, ensuring that your tests comprehensively cover different code paths within your functions.

Let's take an example to illustrate this concept. Consider a function **Get-User** that returns different results for different usernames as shown in Listing 9-17.

Listing 9-17. The sample Get-User function

```
Function Get-User {
    param (
        [string]$username
    )
```

```
    if ($username -eq 'admin') {
        return 'Admin User'
    } else {
        return 'Regular User'
    }
}
```

The accompanying tests shown in Listing 9-18 use mocks with parameter filters to control the function's behavior based on input parameters.

Listing 9-18. Using -ParameterFilter

```
Describe Get-User {
    Context "When getting user information" {
        beforeall {
            mock Get-User {throw "Don't call Get-User ⤷
            for real" }
        }

        it "Should return Admin User for 'admin'" {
            # Arrange
            Mock Get-User {
                return 'Admin User'
            } -ParameterFilter { $username -eq 'admin' }

            # Act
            $result = Get-User -username 'admin'

            # Assert
            $result | Should -Be 'Admin User'
        }

        it "Should return Regular User for other usernames" {
            # Arrange
```

```
Mock Get-User {
    return 'Regular User'
} -ParameterFilter { $username -eq 'Joe' }

# Act
$result = Get-User -username 'Joe'

# Assert
$result | Should -Be 'Regular User'
        }
    }
}
```

In the provided example, the tests could pass without the -ParameterFilter. However, the real power of -ParameterFilter becomes evident in more complex scenarios where the function's behavior hinges on specific parameter values. Here, the filter ensures that the mock is called only when the function is invoked with specific parameters, allowing you to thoroughly test your code's different pathways.

Gotta Catch 'em All

It's important to highlight the 'Catch All' mechanism for mocks, implemented in the **BeforeAll** block. This catch-all prevents unexpected behaviors by intercepting function calls with parameters that don't meet the criteria set by the -ParameterFilter.

Without this catch-all, if a function call doesn't satisfy the filter conditions, the mock won't be invoked, and the real function will be called instead. This safeguard ensures your tests remain robust even in complex scenarios, preventing inadvertent calls to the actual functions being mocked.

For instance, let's consider a modification in our tests. If we alter the second **It** block to call the function: Get-User -username 'Joe' (as shown in Listing 9-19), it doesn't align with the parameter filter's condition of $Username -eq 'Fred'. Consequently, the mock won't be invoked in this case. Instead, the real function will be called, a situation that might not align with your testing objectives.

This highlights the precision that -ParameterFilter offers in selectively mocking specific function calls based on the specified parameter conditions. The 'Catch All' mechanism in the **BeforeAll** block becomes crucial here, ensuring that unexpected calls to the actual functions being mocked are prevented, thereby maintaining the integrity of your tests.

Listing 9-19. The real Get-User is called

```
Describe Get-User {
    Context "When getting user information" {
        beforeall {
            mock Get-User {throw "Don't call Get-User ⤦
            for real" }
        }

        it "Should return Admin User for 'admin'" {
            # Arrange
            Mock Get-User {
                return 'Admin User'
            } -ParameterFilter { $username -eq 'admin' }

            # Act
            $result = Get-User -username 'admin'
```

```
    # Assert
    $result | Should -Be 'Admin User'
}

it "Should return Regular User for other usernames" {
    # Arrange
    Mock Get-User {
        return 'Regular User'
    } -ParameterFilter { $username -eq 'Fred' }

    # Act
    $result = Get-User -username 'Joe'

    # Assert
    $result | Should -Be 'Regular User'
    }
  }
}
```

In Figure 9-2 you can observe the 'Catch All' mechanism in action. Here, the parameter filter set for the **Get-User** function is not met (as shown in the modified test: Listing 9-19), causing the mock to be bypassed. Instead, our safety-net is invoked, triggering the error message specified in the 'Catch All' block. This highlights the importance of the 'Catch All' in maintaining the expected behavior of your tests.

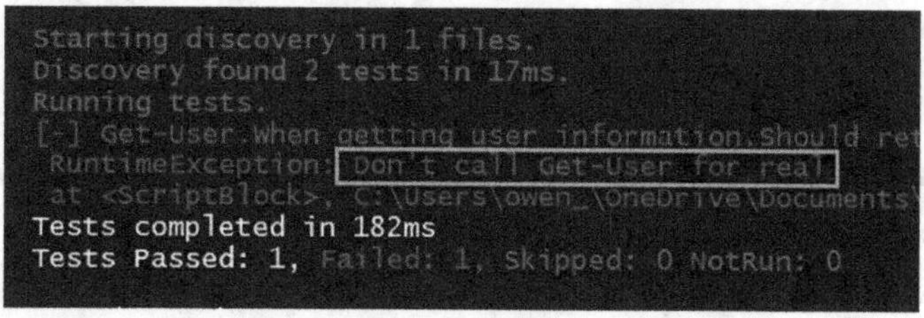

Figure 9-2. *A close shave – saved by the catch all!*

Validating Output Messages Like a Boss Using -ParameterFilter

When you are testing, ensuring the accuracy of output messages, especially those generated by commands like **Write-Host**, **Write-Output**, or **Write-Warning**, is crucial.

This is where the powerful -ParameterFilter parameter in Pester's Mock command steps in. Consider the scenario of a function, **Get-Greeting**, which employs Write-Host to display tailored messages based on input parameters. Listing 9-20 demonstrates this.

Listing 9-20. The sample function

```
Function Get-Greeting {
    param (
        [string]$Name
    )

    if ($Name -eq "Owen") {
        Write-Host "Hello Owen, I hope you are having a ↵
        good day." -ForegroundColor Green
    } else {
        write-Warning "Oh, I see you are not Owen"
        Write-Host "Hello $Name, how are you?" -ForegroundColor
        Cyan
    }
}
```

In the accompanying Pester test shown in Listing 9-21, we utilize -ParameterFilter to scrutinize the exact parameters passed to **Write-Host**.

Listing 9-21. The tests for Get-Greeting

```
Describe "Get-Greeting" {

    Context "When the name is Owen" {
        It "Should say hello to Owen" {

            # Arrange
            Mock Write-Host { }
            $Name = 'Owen'

            # Act
            Get-Greeting -Name $name

            # Assert
            Should -Invoke Write-Host -ParameterFilter ↵
            { $Object -eq "Hello Owen, I hope you are having a
            ↵ good day." }
        }
    }

    Context "When the name is not Owen" {

        It "Should say hello to the name" {

            # Arrange
            Mock Write-Host { }
            Mock Write-Warning { }
            $Name = 'Bob'

            # Act
            Get-Greeting -Name $Name

            # Assert
            Should -Invoke Write-Host -ParameterFilter ↵
            { $Object -eq "Hello $Name, how are you?" ↵
            -and $ForegroundColor -eq "Cyan" }
```

```
            }
        }
    }
```

In the first context block, our focus is on verifying the correctness of the displayed message. In the second context, not only do we validate the message, but we also ensure the accuracy of the foreground color parameter, enhancing the precision of our tests.

This technique is particularly handy when dealing with scenarios where refactoring the code is challenging due to various constraints as you can simply add a `Write-Verbose` or `Write-Host` message and check for the correct message to verify correct code branching. Useful if you have nothing else to assert on.

Imagine your code as a vast, unpredictable sea, each function call being like a message in a bottle. Sometimes, you need to ensure these messages are delivered correctly and in the right bottle. Now, think of the `-ParameterFilter` as a seasoned sailor's compass. In the vast expanse of the code sea, it acts as your reliable navigation tool, helping you pinpoint not just the bottle but also the exact message inside it. Just as a sailor uses a compass to follow a specific route across stormy waters, `-ParameterFilter` allows you to precisely chart the path of your function calls amid the complexities of your code.

It's not just about finding the bottles; it's about ensuring each message reaches its destination flawlessly. Like a skilled navigator using the compass to avoid treacherous rocks, you use `-ParameterFilter` to steer clear of unexpected errors and ambiguities in your tests. In the sea of coding uncertainties, `-ParameterFilter` becomes your guiding star, ensuring your messages are not lost at sea but reach their intended recipients with utmost accuracy and clarity.

> **Note**   I realize the last few analogies are all over the place now, but I have to admit that this far into the book I'm fast running out of theater analogy ideas! From now on, it's a free-for-all in the analogy department; it was good while it lasted!

Verifiable Mocks

In the dynamic world of PowerShell scripting, the reliability of your functions is paramount. Verifiable Mocks, a powerful technique in Pester, serve as vigilant sentinels, ensuring each function's pivotal role in the script. By appending the -Verifiable badge, these mocks become discerning critics, validating the script's execution. Let's delve into this technique, exploring how these mocks guarantee that every function takes its rightful place on the coding stage.

Ensuring the Right Performers Take the Stage

When coding, ensuring that each function plays its part correctly is paramount. I've previously mentioned the use of should -invoke with cmdlets like Write-Host and Write-Verbose, complemented by the discerning -ParameterFilter. This technique becomes invaluable when you need to guarantee that your code follows the expected logic path, triggering the precise Write-Host or Write-Verbose messages.

A critical practice I employ involves orchestrating this validation during the preparation phase of our "theatrical performance," shifting the focus from the Assert section to the Arrange section of our test. Here, our mock functions transition from mere observers to active participants. We bestow upon them the responsibility of validation by appending the -Verifiable parameter. This essential role, akin to a vigilant theater critic, ensures that specific functions are called precisely as anticipated.

Consider the script demonstrated in Listing 9-22 that stages the interaction between our code and two crucial performers, Write-Host and Write-Warning.

Listing 9-22. Invoke-Verifiable at large

```
Describe "Get-Greeting" {

    Context "When the name is Owen" {
        It "Should say hello to Owen" {

            # Arrange
            Mock Write-Host -ParameterFilter { $Object ⤸
            -eq "Hello Owen, I hope you are having a good day."
            } ⤸ -Verifiable

            # Act
            Get-Greeting -Name "Owen"

            # Assert
            Should -InvokeVerifiable
        }
    }

    Context "When the name is not Owen" {

        It "Should say hello to the name" {

            # Arrange
            Mock Write-Warning { } -ParameterFilter ⤸
            { $Message -eq "Oh, I see you are not Owen" }
            -Verifiable
            Mock Write-Host { } -ParameterFilter
            { $Object ⤸-eq "Hello $Name, how are you?" -and
            $ForegroundColor -eq "Cyan" } -Verifiable
            $Name = 'Bob'
```

```
# Act
Get-Greeting -Name $Name

# Assert
Should -InvokeVerifiable

        }
    }
}
```

In the first act (context block) when the protagonist's name is "Owen", we scrutinize whether the correct message is displayed. Our mock function for Write-Host is marked as Verifiable by appending -Verifiable to the end of the mock, affirming its importance in our performance.

In the second act (context block), when our protagonist takes a different identity, the same level of scrutiny is applied. Here, we validate not only the message but also the foreground color, demonstrating the nuanced capabilities of -ParameterFilter in tandem with -Verifiable. Additionally, Write-Warning is treated with the same -Verifiable parameter.

The validation occurs seamlessly in the Assert section, where the should -InvokeVerifiable scrutinizes the mock's execution. It will check that every mock with -Verifiable tacked on to the end has been correctly called and, if not, will fail the test.

Moreover, the beauty of this approach lies in its efficiency. With just one line of code, you can verify all your mocks at once, in our example, all three, ensuring a comprehensive and robust evaluation of your script's performance.

Verifiable Mocks also shine when we want to ensure the invocation of functions that we don't necessarily want to test. For instance, imagine a function responsible for sending emails or writing to a log file. We might not want to delve into their intricacies, but we certainly want to guarantee their execution. Enter the power of Verifiable Mocks. By appending the

-Verifiable switch to our mock commands, we command Pester to scrutinize their performance. The subsequent should -InvokeVerifiable in the Assert phase of the test then becomes our discerning audience, ensuring that the functions took their rightful place on the stage.

Caution   without a -ParameterFilter, should -InvokeVerifiable will pass if the mock is called once or more times. While this grants flexibility, it might compromise accuracy. Thus, striking a balance between flexibility and precision becomes a vital consideration in your testing scripts.

In essence, Verifiable Mocks are the watchful guardians of your code, ensuring that each function steps into the limelight as expected. By bestowing upon them the -Verifiable badge, you guarantee not just code execution but an orchestrated performance that adheres to your script's grand design. The theater of coding, with its splendid actors and vigilant critics, truly comes to life with the power of Verifiable Mocks.

Mocking Without Modules: Ensuring Test Portability

Ensuring your tests run seamlessly across different environments is crucial. Yet, when it comes to mocking functions or cmdlets that rely on specific modules or tools, guaranteeing this portability can be challenging. Picture this: your tests run smoothly on your computer, where all the necessary modules are installed, but the moment someone else attempts to run them, or they are integrated into an automated CI/CD pipeline, disaster strikes – the tests fail.

Pester, in its wisdom, creates mock versions of functions or cmdlets, expecting them to be present on the testing machine. This becomes problematic when the tests are executed in environments lacking the required modules. So how do you ensure your tests don't fail in these scenarios? The solution lies in creating a simplified version of the required function or cmdlet directly within your Pester test.

Consider this scenario: you're testing a function called **Get-ADUserDisabledState.** This function interacts with **Get-ADUser**, a cmdlet from the Active Directory module. Listing 9-23 shows this function.

Listing 9-23. The sample Get-ADUserDisabledState function

```
Function Get-ADUserDisabledState {
    param (
        [bool]$State = $false
    )

    $users = @(Get-Aduser -Filter {Enabled -eq $State} ↪
    -SearchBase = 'OU=Users,OU=MyCompany,DC=OH,DC-Local')

    if ($state -eq $false) {
        Write-Host "There are $($users.Count) disabled ↪
        user accounts:"
        $users.name
    } else {
        Write-Host "There are $($users.Count) enabled ↪
        user accounts:"
        $users.name
    }
}
```

To guarantee test portability, you recreate **Get-ADUser** within your test environment.

Before writing the test, I used **GetType** against the results of Get-ADUser to see what type of object was used to return the data as shown in Figure 9-3 and Figure 9-4.

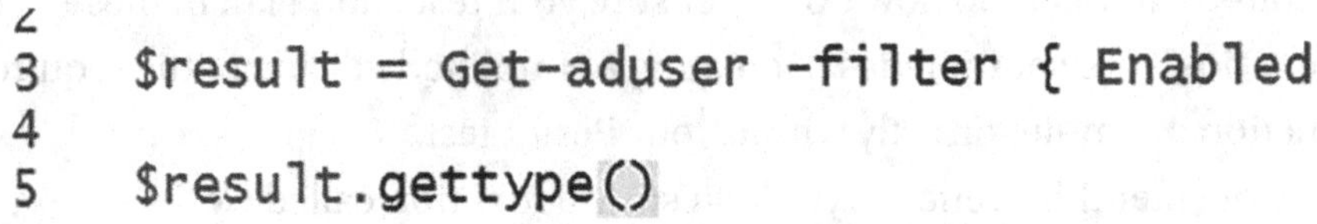

```
2
3    $result = Get-aduser -filter { Enabled
4
5    $result.gettype()
```

Figure 9-3. *Using GetType to determine the returned object*

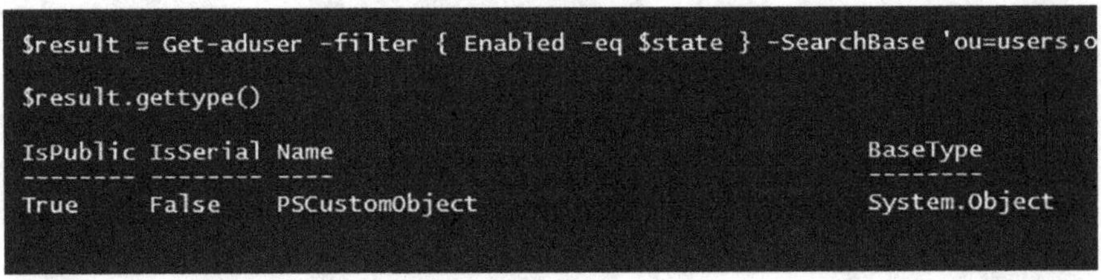

```
$result = Get-aduser -filter { Enabled -eq $state } -SearchBase 'ou=users,o
$result.gettype()

IsPublic IsSerial Name                                    BaseType
-------- -------- ----                                    --------
True     False    PSCustomObject                          System.Object
```

Figure 9-4. *It's a PSCustomObject!*

So I'll mock with a PSCustom object too. Listing 9-24 shows what the tests looks like initially.

Listing 9-24. Well, it worked on my computer!

```
Describe "Get-ADUserDisabledState" {

    Context "When the user is disabled" {
        It "Should return the disabled user" {
            # Arrange
            mock Get-ADUser {
                [PSCustomObject]@{
                    Name = "Test User1"
```

```
                    Enabled = $false
            }
        }

    # Act
    $expected = Get-ADUserDisabledState -State $false

    # Assert
    $expected | Should -Be "Test User1"
    }
}

Context "When the user is enabled" {
    It "Should return the enabled user" {
        # Arrange
        mock Get-ADUser {
            [PSCustomObject]@{
                Name = "Test User2"
                Enabled = $True
            }
        }

        # Act
        $expected = Get-ADUserDisabledState -State $true

        #Assert
        $expected | Should -Be "Test User2"
    }
  }
}
```

If I run the test on a system that does not have access to **Get-ADUser**, the test fails (Figure 9-5). And tells you in no uncertain terms, "Could not find Command Get-ADuser"

```
Starting discovery in 1 files.
Discovery found 1 tests in 1.19s.
Running tests.
[-] Get-ADUserDisabledState.When the user is disabled.Should re
  CommandNotFoundException: Could not find Command Get-ADUser
Tests completed in 6.11s
Tests Passed: 0, Failed: 1, Skipped: 0 NotRun: 0
```

Figure 9-5. *The test failed because the AD cmdlets were not installed on this computer*

The solution is to define a blank function of the same name within your test, as demonstrated by Listing 9-25, within the **BeforeAll** script block.

Listing 9-25. It's an easy solution, simply define a blank function

```
Describe "Get-ADUserDisabledState" {
    beforeAll {
        Function Get-ADUser {}

        Mock Write-Host {}
    }

    Context "When the user is disabled" {
        It "Should return the disabled user" {
            # Arrange
            mock Get-ADUser {
                [PSCustomObject]@{
                    Name = "Test User1"
                    Enabled = $false
                }
            }

            # Act
            $expected = Get-ADUserDisabledState -State $false
```

```
        # Assert
        $expected | Should -Be "Test User1"
    }
}

Context "When the user is enabled" {
    It "Should return the enabled user" {
        # Arrange
        mock Get-ADUser {
            [PSCustomObject]@{
                Name = "Test User2"
                Enabled = $True
            }
        }

        # Act
        $expected = Get-ADUserDisabledState -State $true

        #Assert
        $expected | Should -Be "Test User2"
    }
}
}
```

Figure 9-6 now shows the results of the "dummy" function: the test suite passes with flying colors.

```
Running tests from 'C:\Users\owen_\OneDr
Describing Get-ADUserDisabledState
 Context When the user is disabled
     [+] Should return the disabled user 1
 Context When the user is enabled
     [+] Should return the enabled user 22
Tests completed in 459ms
Tests Passed: 2, Failed: 0, Skipped: 0 N
```

Figure 9-6. The test passes even though Get-ADUser is not installed on the computer

By simulating the necessary functions directly within your test, you ensure that the tests remain robust and functional, regardless of the absence of specific modules in different environments. This technique ensures your tests are not just reliable on your machine but are also ready to perform flawlessly on any stage, ensuring the integrity of your code across diverse settings.

Mocking with Modules: Navigating Module Scopes

Modules, the building blocks of PowerShell's modular architecture, often contain a mix of public and private functions. Testing these modules, especially the private functions, presents a unique challenge. Consider a scenario where a module defines a private function internally used by a public function. How do you mock this private function for testing purposes?

In our example module, seen in Listing 9-26, the public function **Get-UpperCase** internally calls the private function **ConvertTo-UpperCase** to perform its task.

Listing 9-26. Our sample module that calls a private function

```
Function ConvertTo-UpperCase {
    param (
        [string]$text
    )

    return $text.ToUpper()
}

Function Get-UpperCase {
    param (
        [string]$Text
    )

    return ConvertTo-UpperCase -text $Text
}

Export-ModuleMember -Function Get-UpperCase
```

When attempting to mock the private function without specifying its module context as shown in Listing 9-27, your test might fail to locate the function, leading to unexpected results.

Listing 9-27. The test fails to locate the private function

```
BeforeAll {
    Import-Module "$PSScriptRoot\Mock_module01.psm1" ↩
    -Force -PassThru
}

Describe "Get-Uppercase" {
    It "should return uppercase text" {

        mock ConvertTo-Uppercase -MockWith {"HELLO"}

        $expected = Get-UpperCase -Text "hello"
```

```
    $expected | should -be "HELLO"

  }
}
```

Figure 9-7 shows the results of executing Listing 9-27.

```
Starting discovery in 1 files.
Discovery found 1 tests in 18ms.
Running tests.
[-] Get-Uppercase.should return uppercase text 67ms  (66ms|1ms)
 CommandNotFoundException: Could not find Command ConvertTo-Uppercase
Tests completed in 150ms
Tests Passed: 0, Failed: 1, Skipped: 0 NotRun: 0
```

Figure 9-7. *The test fails – it could not find the private function "ConvertTo-UpperCase"*

Two common approaches to mitigate this is to use the **-ModuleName** parameter or encapsulate the test within an **InModuleScope** script block.

Using the -ModuleName Parameter

By specifying the module name when mocking a private function, you explicitly indicate the module context for the mock. In the test scenario, this approach ensures the mock operates within the correct scope, enabling the test to locate the private function and perform as expected. Not only does this method provide speed advantages, but it also enhances code clarity. You clearly define the module context, making your tests more understandable for both yourself and other developers.

You are only required to add -ModuleName to any **Mock** or **Should -Invoke** commands within your test suite as demonstrated by Listing 9-28.

Listing 9-28. Using -ModuleName for speed and clarity

```
BeforeAll {
    Import-Module "$PSScriptRoot\<moduleName>.psm1" ↵
```

```
-Force -PassThru
}

Describe "Get-Uppercase" {
    It "should return uppercase text" {
        # Arrange
        mock ConvertTo-Uppercase -MockWith {"HELLO"} ↵
        -ModuleName moduleName

        # Act
        $expected = Get-UpperCase -Text "hello"

        # Assert
        $expected | should -be "HELLO"
        should -invoke ConvertTo-UpperCase -times 1 ↵
        -exactly -ModuleName moduleName
    }
}
```

Note   This will only allow you to mock private functions that are called by your public functions. In Listing 9-2 the public function (**Get-Uppercase**) calls the private function (**ConvertTo-Uppercase**). If you wish to write a unit test for a private function directly, you will need to use InModuleScope.

Using InModuleScope Script Block

Alternatively, you can encapsulate your tests within an **InModuleScope** script block. This approach ensures everything inside the block runs within the module scope. However, be cautious, as this method makes both public and private functions in the module available to your tests, potentially leading to undesired consequences. Listing 9-29 demonstrates this approach.

Listing 9-29. Sometimes you have no option but to use InModuleScope

```
BeforeAll {
    Import-Module "$PSScriptRoot\<moduleName>.psm1" ↵
    -Force -PassThru
}

Describe "Get-Uppercase" {

    It "should return uppercase text" {
        InModuleScope  'moduleName' {
            # Arrange
            mock ConvertTo-UpperCase -MockWith {"HELLO"}

            # Act
            $expected = Get-UpperCase -Text "hello"

            # Assert
            $expected | should -be "HELLO"
            should -invoke ConvertTo-UpperCase -times ↵
            1 -exactly
        }
    }
}
```

To follow best practice, you should avoid wrapping **InModuleScope** around your **Describe** or **It** blocks – sure, it can be done, but you will end up slowing down the Discovery Phase and won't ensure that your functions are properly tested.

Note   Using **InModuleScope** has a significant benefit: it provides access to all functions within the module, both public and private. This means you can call a private function in your test script, rather than mock it, even if it hasn't been exported by the module. It's also handy if you need to write a unit test for a private function in the module.

While both methods achieve the goal, using the -**ModuleName** parameter is considered best practice due to its speed, specificity, and clarity advantages. This explicit indication of the module context makes your tests robust, efficient, and easy to comprehend, ensuring the smooth navigation of module scopes during testing.

Summary

While this chapter may have tested your persistence, the invaluable skills you've gained are well worth the effort. You've embarked on a journey into the art of mocking in PowerShell, a fundamental practice for powerful and effective testing. By exploring the sample code, delving into diverse examples, and rereading key concepts, you've equipped yourself with the knowledge to transform how you test your scripts.

Through various examples and scenarios, you've explored the nuances of mocking, from simple function mocks to more complex interactions involving parameters and module scopes.

You've discovered the power of -ParameterFilter in honing your mocks to specific conditions, ensuring precise testing of diverse code paths. You've explored the concept of Verifiable Mocks, vigilant gatekeepers that validate function invocations, bolstering the integrity of your tests. Moreover, you've learned the art of mocking private functions within modules, crucial for testing encapsulated code.

By mastering these techniques, you've gained the power to comprehensively validate your PowerShell scripts. Whether it's simulating specific scenarios, validating complex interactions, or testing encapsulated code, you now possess the tools to elevate your testing game.

Beyond This Chapter

Remember, effective testing is not just about verifying your code; it's about ensuring its robustness under diverse conditions. Mocking empowers you to create controlled environments, simulate various situations, and assess your scripts' behavior with confidence.

Your Journey Continues

Now that you've mastered the art of mocking, are you curious about how much of your code you're actually testing? Dive into the captivating world of code coverage in the next chapter, where we'll unveil techniques to measure and maximize the effectiveness of your test suite. Get ready to unveil hidden corners of your code and ensure its robustness like never before!

CHAPTER 10

Unveiling the Secrets of Code Coverage

By now, you've mastered the art of crafting powerful Pester tests. But have you ever wondered: are you testing all the corners of your code? This is where the intriguing concept of code coverage comes into play.

Imagine having a map that visualizes which areas of your code have been thoroughly tested and identifies any hidden pathways left unexplored. Code coverage gives you just that! In this chapter, you'll embark on a journey to

Demystify code coverage: Understand what it is, why it matters, and the different metrics used to measure it.

Generating insights: Discover how to interpret coverage reports, identify untested areas, and prioritize future testing efforts.

Optimizing tests and code: Utilize insights from coverage data to refine your testing strategy, write targeted tests, and ensure your code is well protected from unseen issues.

By the end of this chapter, you'll understand how to maximize your testing investment and achieve peace of mind knowing your code is robust and ready for any challenge.

© Owen Heaume 2024
O. Heaume, *Getting Started with Pester 5*, https://doi.org/10.1007/979-8-8688-0306-2_10

Demystifying Code Coverage: Unveiling the Map of Your Code's Tested Terrain

Imagine building a magnificent castle, brick by painstaking brick. But how can you be sure every brick is strong and contributes to its overall stability? Code coverage serves as the architect's blueprint, highlighting which areas of your code have been tested and ensuring no hidden weaknesses remain undetected.

In essence, code coverage measures the percentage of your code that is executed during testing. It's like having a map that lights up specific regions when you walk over them, revealing how thoroughly you've explored your code's landscape. But why is this so important?

Well, untested code is like an unexplored path in the wilderness, potentially harboring unexpected pitfalls. High code coverage minimizes the chance of hidden bugs lurking in the shadows, protecting your scripts from unexpected behavior and ensuring reliability. Imagine blindly firing arrows into the darkness hoping to hit the target. Code coverage reports act as spotlights, illuminating areas that haven't been tested, allowing you to prioritize and streamline your testing efforts for maximum impact. Knowing your code is well tested fosters confidence and reduces anxiety. With high coverage, you can sleep soundly knowing you've covered all the bases and your scripts are prepared to handle real-world situations.

Metrics: Unveiling the Degrees of Coverage

Just like maps use different symbols to represent terrain, code coverage utilizes various metrics to gauge your testing comprehensiveness. For instance:

> **Statement coverage:** Tracks the percentage of individual code statements executed during tests.

Branch coverage: Measures how well different decision points (e.g., if-else statements) are exercised by tests.

Function coverage: Ensures each function or method within your code is called at least once during testing.

Remember, a single metric doesn't paint the whole picture. A healthy mix of metrics helps you analyze different aspects of your code's coverage and create a more comprehensive understanding.

Sample Functions and Tests

Before delving into code coverage, let's visit our sample functions: **Compliment-Yourself** and **Compliment-Owen** shown in Listing 10-1.

Listing 10-1. Our sample functions are contained in our Functions.ps1 file

```
function Compliment-Yourself {
    $randomNumber = Get-Random -Minimum 1 -Maximum 3

    if ($randomNumber -eq 1) {
        return 'You are doing great!'
    } else {
        return 'Keep up the good work!'
    }
}

Function Compliment-Owen {
    $randomNumber = Get-Random -Minimum 1 -Maximum 3
```

```
    if ($randomNumber -eq 1) {
        return 'Well done Owen, you are doing great!'
    } elseif ($randomNumber -eq 2) {
        return 'Hey Owen! Keep up the good work!'
    } else {
        return 'This is a great chapter!'
    }
}
```

These functions are accompanied by the Pester tests demonstrated by Listing 10-2.

Listing 10-2. The pester tests: our Functions.tests.ps1 file

```
beforeall {
    . "$psscriptroot\Functions.ps1"
}

Describe 'Testing Compliment-Yourself and Compliment-Owen' {
    It 'Compliments yourself with "You are doing great!"' {
        # Mocking the random number to ensure the ↵
        specific branch is tested
        Mock Get-Random { 1 }
        $result = Compliment-Yourself
        $result | Should -Be 'You are doing great!'

    }

    It 'Compliments Owen with " Well done Owen, ↵
    You are doing great!"' {
        # Mocking the random number to ensure the ↵
        specific branch is tested
        Mock Get-Random { 1 }
        $result = Compliment-Owen
```

```
    $result | Should -Be 'Well done Owen, you ↳
    are doing great!'
  }
}
```

Now, let's see what code coverage can do for us in helping to identify areas for testing improvement by creating our configuration file.

Pester Code Coverage Configuration

Configuring a Pester configuration file is our first step. In Listing 10-3, we leverage New-PesterConfiguration to specify the path to our test file and activate code coverage. We've saved this separate file as Test.ps1.

Listing 10-3. Our Pester Code Coverage Configuration Item saved as Test.ps1

```
$config = New-PesterConfiguration
$config.Run.Path = ".\src\Functions.tests.ps1"
$config.CodeCoverage.Enabled = $true

Invoke-Pester -Configuration $config
```

Let's take a moment and walk through step-by-step what we've just done.

Step 1: Utilizing New-PesterConfiguration

The core of your configuration endeavors lies in the New-PesterConfiguration cmdlet. This command sets the stage for defining how Pester should conduct its tests, including the critical aspect of code coverage.

```
# Creating a new Pester configuration object
$config = New-PesterConfiguration
```

This command initializes a configuration object, a bit like creating a blueprint that informs Pester exactly what to do. Think of it as the master plan for orchestrating your tests, ensuring they align with your specific needs and goals.

Step 2: Setting the Test File Path

With the configuration object in hand, the next step is to specify the path to your test file. This ensures Pester knows exactly where to find and execute the tests. The Run.Path property serves this purpose.

```
# Setting the path to the test file
$config.Run.Path = ".\src\Functions.tests.ps1"
```

By defining the test file path, you're providing Pester with a roadmap to navigate through your tests and execute them systematically.

Step 3: Activating Code Coverage

Now comes the pivotal moment – activating code coverage.

```
# Activating code coverage
$config.CodeCoverage.Enabled = $true
```

When you enable CodeCoverage.Enabled, you're telling Pester to unlock a whole new level of insight into your code – it's like giving it a map to explore every line that your tests touch.

Step 4: Invoking Pester with the Configuration

Finally, the Invoke-Pester cmdlet, coupled with your configuration object, is the catalyst for initiating the testing process.

```
# Invoking Pester with the configuration
Invoke-Pester -Configuration $config
```

This command kicks off the testing journey, leveraging the detailed configuration you've constructed. Pester now traverses through your tests, executes them, and, thanks to code coverage activation, provides insights into how thoroughly your code is being tested.

Running the Configuration

Now we have our configuration file saved as Test.ps1, we can run it. Doing so will execute our tests as well as present us with some code coverage metrics as shown in Figure 10-1.

```
PS C:\ohtemp\cc3> C:\OHTemp\cc3\Test.ps1
Starting discovery in 1 files.
Discovery found 2 tests in 8ms.
Starting code coverage.
Running tests.
[+] C:\ohtemp\cc3\src\Functions.tests.ps1 111ms (36ms|69ms)
Tests completed in 114ms
Tests Passed: 2, Failed: 0, Skipped: 0 NotRun: 0
Processing code coverage result.
Covered 60% / 75%. 10 analyzed Commands in 1 File.
```

Figure 10-1. *Code coverage metrics*

Breaking Down the Metrics

By default, the code coverage configuration employs a 75% threshold for the amount of code that needs to be covered for a successful pass. In the current report, we've attained a coverage rate of 60% against this 75% benchmark. Clearly, there is room for enhancement in our testing efforts!

On closer inspection of the **Functions.tests.ps1** file we can see we inadvertently forgot to test for this particular section of code in our **Compliment-Owen** function:

```
...elseif ($randomNumber -eq 2) {
        return 'Hey Owen! Keep up the good work!' ...
```

Let's fix this and add a test for it. Listing 10-4 shows the revised
.tests file.

Listing 10-4. Adding a new test for better code coverage

```
beforeall {
    . "$psscriptroot\Functions.ps1"
}
Describe 'Testing Compliment-Yourself and Compliment-Owen' {
    It 'Compliments yourself with "You are doing great!"' {
        # Mocking the random number to ensure the ↻
        specific branch is tested
        Mock Get-Random { 1 }
        $result = Compliment-Yourself
        $result | Should -Be 'You are doing great!'

    }

    It 'Compliments Owen with " Well done Owen, ↻You are doing
    great!"' {
        # Mocking the random number to ensure the ↻
        specific branch is tested
        Mock Get-Random { 1 }
        $result = Compliment-Owen
        $result | Should -Be 'Well done Owen, you are ↻
        doing great!'
    }
    It 'Compliments Owen with "Hey Owen! Keep up the ↻
    good work!"' {
        # Mocking the random number to ensure the ↻
        specific branch is tested
        Mock Get-Random { 2 }
```

```
    $result = Compliment-Owen
    $result | Should -Be 'Hey Owen! Keep up the ↩
    good work!'
  }
}
```

Executing our Pester configuration file for code coverage now reveals the ensuing metrics, as depicted in Figure 10-2.

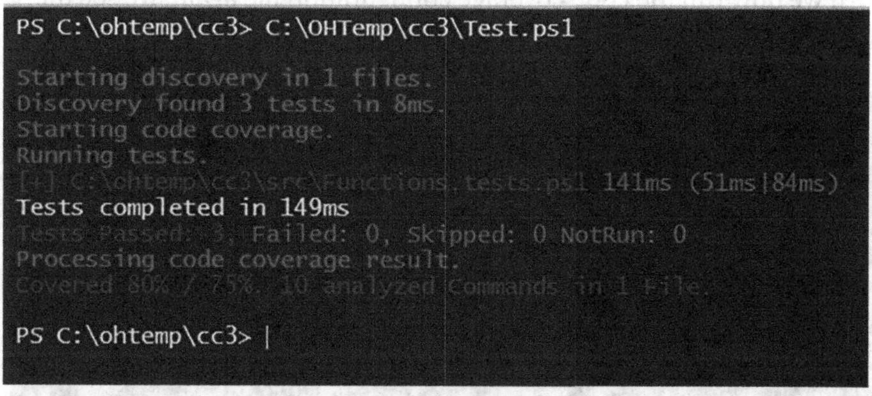

```
PS C:\ohtemp\cc3> C:\OHTemp\cc3\Test.ps1
Starting discovery in 1 files.
Discovery found 3 tests in 8ms.
Starting code coverage.
Running tests.
[+] C:\ohtemp\cc3\src\Functions.tests.ps1 141ms (51ms|84ms)
Tests completed in 149ms
Tests Passed: 3, Failed: 0, Skipped: 0 NotRun: 0
Processing code coverage result.
Covered 80% / 75%. 10 analyzed Commands in 1 File.

PS C:\ohtemp\cc3> |
```

Figure 10-2. *Success! We have green lights!*

Fantastic news! We've reached an impressive 80% of our initial 75% target. However, aiming higher, I prefer a 90% code coverage. To accomplish this, we can elevate our aspirations by including the following line in our Pester Configuration file:

`$config.CodeCoverage.CoveragePercentTarget = 90`

With this addition, we are now striving to achieve a commendable 90% code coverage as demonstrated in Listing 10-5.

Listing 10-5. Setting the target code coverage to 90%

```
$config = New-PesterConfiguration
$config.Run.Path = ".\src\Functions.tests.ps1"
$config.CodeCoverage.Enabled = $true
$config.CodeCoverage.CoveragePercentTarget = 90

Invoke-Pester -Configuration $config
```

If we now run the code coverage configuration file again, we see the following metrics as shown in Figure 10-3.

```
PS C:\ohtemp\cc3> C:\OHTemp\cc3\Test.ps1
Starting discovery in 1 files.
Discovery found 3 tests in 10ms.
Starting code coverage.
Running tests.
[+] C:\ohtemp\cc3\src\Functions.tests.ps1 122ms (51ms|65ms)
Tests completed in 127ms
Tests Passed: 3, Failed: 0, Skipped: 0 NotRun: 0
Processing code coverage result.
Covered 80% / 90%. 10 analyzed Commands in 1 File.

PS C:\ohtemp\cc3>
```

Figure 10-3. *We are now 10% shy of our target*

With the current coverage standing at 80%, there's a remaining 10% to fulfill our target. To pinpoint precisely what areas we've missed in our tests, let's introduce an additional line to our Pester configuration file:

```
$config.Output.Verbosity = "Detailed"
```

This adjustment enhances the verbosity of our output, providing detailed insights into the areas that require further testing to meet our ambitious 90% code coverage target. Listing 10-6 shows the configuration file with our new addition.

Listing 10-6. The new Pester configuration file

```
$config = New-PesterConfiguration
$config.Run.Path = ".\src\Functions.tests.ps1"
$config.CodeCoverage.Enabled = $true
$config.CodeCoverage.CoveragePercentTarget = 90
$config.Output.Verbosity = "Detailed"

Invoke-Pester -Configuration $config
```

Running our configuration file now gives us the following metrics as shown in Figure 10-4.

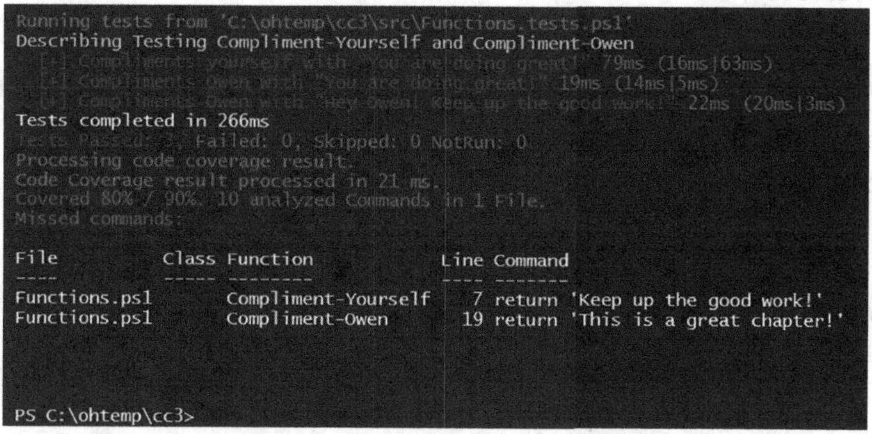

Figure 10-4. *Detailed metrics*

Indeed, the decision to elevate the verbosity level to "Detailed" proves to be an excellent move. This adjustment not only provides a more intricate view of our test results but also illuminates exactly what has been overlooked in our tests. The metrics now clearly indicate that line 7 in the **Compliment-Yourself** function and line 19 in the **Compliment-Owen** function were not executed under any of the tests within our test suite.

With this detailed information, we can discern which functions, the specific line numbers, and precisely what needs to be tested to address the gaps in our coverage.

Listing 10-7 proudly showcases our refined .tests file, adorned with the latest additions to our test suite. These new tests have been carefully incorporated to address the areas we previously missed, as highlighted by the detailed insights gleaned from our code coverage metrics.

Listing 10-7. Two new tests have been added, one for each function as identified by the code coverage metrics

```
beforeall {
    . "$psscriptroot\Functions.ps1"
}

Describe 'Testing Compliment-Yourself and ↳
Compliment-Owen function' {

    It 'Compliments yourself with "You are doing great!"' {
        # Mocking the random number to ensure the ↳
        specific branch is tested
        Mock Get-Random { 1 }
        $result = Compliment-Yourself
        $result | Should -Be 'You are doing great!'
    }

    It 'Compliments yourself with "Keep up the good work!"' {
        # Mocking the random number to ensure the ↳
        specific branch is tested
        Mock Get-Random { 2 }
        $result = Compliment-Yourself
        $result | Should -Be 'Keep up the good work!'
    }
```

```
It 'Compliments Owen with "Well done Owen, ↵
you are doing great!"' {
    # Mocking the random number to ensure the ↵
    specific branch is tested
    Mock Get-Random { 1 }
    $result = Compliment-Owen
    $result | Should -Be 'Well done Owen, ↵
    you are doing great!'
}

It 'Compliments Owen with "Hey Owen! ↵
Keep up the good work!"' {
    # Mocking the random number to ensure the ↵
    specific branch is tested
    Mock Get-Random { 2 }
    $result = Compliment-Owen
    $result | Should -Be 'Hey Owen! Keep up ↵
    the good work!'
}

It 'Compliments Owen with "This is a great chapter!"' {
    # Mocking the random number to ensure the ↵
    specific branch is tested
    Mock Get-Random { 3 }
    $result = Compliment-Owen
    $result | Should -Be 'This is a great chapter!'
}
}
```

Each line in this revised file is a testament to our commitment to thorough testing.

If we run the code coverage configuration once more, we are presented with the metrics as shown in Figure 10-5.

```
PS C:\ohtemp\cc3> C:\OHTemp\cc3\Test.ps1
Pester v5.5.0

Starting discovery in 1 files.
Discovery found 5 tests in 31ms.
Starting code coverage.
Code Coverage preparation finished after 30 ms.
Running tests.

Running tests from 'Functions.tests.ps1'
Describing Testing Compliment-Yourself and Compliment
    [+] Compliments yourself with "You are doing great!
    [+] Compliments yourself with "Keep up the good wor
    [+] Compliments Owen with "Well done Owen, you are
    [+] Compliments Owen with "Hey Owen! Keep up the go
    [+] Compliments Owen with "This is a great chapter!
Tests completed in 356ms
Tests Passed: 5, Failed: 0, Skipped: 0 NotRun: 0
Processing code coverage result.
Code Coverage result processed in 52 ms.
Covered 100% / 90%. 10 analyzed Commands in 1 File.
```

Figure 10-5. *We have 100% code coverage!*

Triumphant news! We've achieved the pinnacle of success – a perfect 100%! This stellar outcome surpasses our initial target of 90%, signifying that every nook and cranny of our code has been thoroughly covered by our tests.

Best Practices for Code Coverage Targets

There isn't a universally defined "best practice" percentage for code coverage targets in Pester or any other testing framework. The appropriate target for code coverage can vary based on the specific needs and goals of a project, team, or organization.

Some projects may aim for a high code coverage target, such as 90% or more, to ensure a comprehensive set of tests covers most of the codebase. This can be particularly important in safety-critical systems or environments with stringent quality assurance requirements.

On the other hand, some projects may find a lower code coverage target, like the default 75% set by Pester, to be sufficient. I saw a video with Pester maintainer Jakub Jares where he was asked his thoughts on what the ideal percentage should be. He replied 75%, which is why it is the default setting. For me personally, this is too low, and in my workplace, we have this set at 90%, but it does nicely demonstrate how there really is no perfect number; it truly is different for all. Remember though, setting a realistic and achievable code coverage target is crucial, as overly ambitious targets can lead to diminishing returns and unnecessary efforts in some cases.

Running Coverage Across a Directory

Previously, we pointed $Config.Run.Path to a specific .tests file. But what if you have multiple test files in a directory? No sweat! Simply update the path to encompass the entire root directory:

```
$config.Run.Path = ".\code"
```

Alternatively, achieve the same result with

```
$config.CodeCoverage.Path
```

This will override the path from the general settings if present. Listing 10-8 shows our revised configuration file.

Listing 10-8. The revised configuration file now points to a root directory for our tests and code to be tested

```
$config = New-PesterConfiguration
$config.CodeCoverage.Enabled = $true
$config.CodeCoverage.CoveragePercentTarget = 90
$config.Output.Verbosity = "Detailed"
$config.CodeCoverage.Path = ".\src"

Invoke-Pester -Configuration $config
```

Important   Keep your configuration file separate from your test files. If they share the same directory, Pester may attempt to include code coverage metrics on itself, leading to unintended consequences.

Now, when you execute your configuration file, Pester will scan all .tests files within the **.\src** directory and generate a comprehensive coverage report encompassing your entire codebase. This way, you can ensure all your functions and scripts are thoroughly tested without manually specifying each file path.

Understanding Pester's Coverage.xml

Every time you run a code coverage check, Pester graciously generates a coverage.xml file. This XML file is more than just a file; it's a treasure trove of information about your test results. Think of it as a detailed report, documenting which parts of your code were tested and how thoroughly.

Why XML?

XML (eXtensible Markup Language) is a versatile and human-readable format that represents structured data. In the context of Pester, the coverage.xml file serves as a standardized way to communicate your test results. This file can be understood not only by humans but also by external tools or programs designed to analyze and visualize test coverage.

How Can You Use It?

Imagine having a tool that visualizes your test coverage, highlights untested areas, or integrates with your continuous integration pipeline. (You will see how we can integrate CodeCoverage in Azure DevOps using this file in Chapter 11.) The coverage.xml file enables exactly that. External tools or programs can read this file and provide insights in a more easily readable way.

Customizing Output Path

If you prefer the coverage.xml file to reside in a specific location, you can customize the output path using $config.CodeCoverage.OutputPath in your configuration file. For example:

```
$config.CodeCoverage.OutputPath = "path\to\coverage.xml"
```

In essence, the coverage.xml file is your gateway to deeper insights and collaboration with external tools to enhance your testing workflow.

Exploring Pester Configuration

In the journey of mastering Pester, the configuration file emerges as a potent ally. Not only is it instrumental in shaping code coverage parameters, but it also harbors a wealth of features that extend beyond just code coverage analysis. Let's take a brief look at the Pester configuration file and how you can unravel its capabilities.

Creating the Pester Configuration File

The Pester configuration file is your command center, orchestrating how tests are executed and providing valuable insights into various testing aspects. In our example at the start of the chapter, we created a configuration file using the command

```
$config = New-PesterConfiguration
```

This simple line lays the foundation for a dynamic configuration object named $config, which encapsulates the settings governing your tests.

Diving into Configuration Options

Once your configuration file is in place, the exploration begins. You can gain a comprehensive overview of available options by typing $config in the console as shown in Figure 10-6. (Remember, $config is just a variable – you can name it anything you like.)

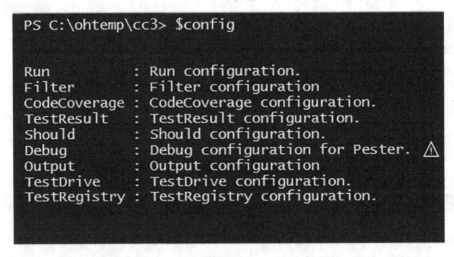

Figure 10-6. Exploring your configuration object

Executing this command in your console reveals a plethora of parameters encapsulated within the configuration object. It's like having a control panel at your fingertips, allowing you to fine-tune your testing environment.

Drilling Down into Specific Parameters

Suppose you're eager to delve deeper into a particular aspect, let's pick **CodeCoverage** from the displayed list. To unravel the mysteries hidden within this facet of the configuration, you simply type $config. CodeCoverage as depicted in Figure 10-7.

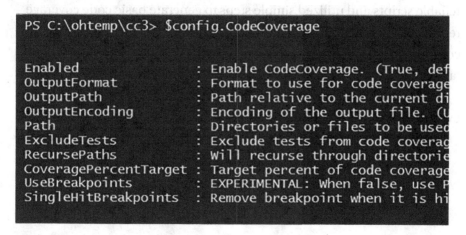

```
PS C:\ohtemp\cc3> $config.CodeCoverage

Enabled                 : Enable CodeCoverage. (True, def
OutputFormat            : Format to use for code coverage
OutputPath              : Path relative to the current di
OutputEncoding          : Encoding of the output file. (U
Path                    : Directories or files to be used
ExcludeTests            : Exclude tests from code coverag
RecursePaths            : Will recurse through directorie
CoveragePercentTarget   : Target percent of code coverage
UseBreakpoints          : EXPERIMENTAL: When false, use F
SingleHitBreakpoints    : Remove breakpoint when it is hi
```

Figure 10-7. Drilling deeper into the configuration object, each item has its own line of help text

Using this dot notation to access CodeCoverage provides a view of all parameters associated with it. From coverage percent targets to output paths, every nuance is at your disposal for customization.

The beauty of the Pester configuration lies in its versatility. Beyond code coverage, you can configure all sorts of aspects, and as you embark on this exploration, remember that learning about each parameter empowers you to tailor your testing environment according to the unique needs of your scripts and projects. Take a few minutes to explore and try out some of these configuration options – even if you don't use them now, understanding what is available and how they work will elevate your game in the long term.

Summary

In this chapter, we demystified code coverage and harnessed its power using a Pester configuration file.

We explored why testing every code corner matters for robust and reliable scripts and utilized simple steps to generate basic code coverage reports. You learned how to tailor reports and set specific targets for coverage goals and finally saw how to identify untested areas and write targeted tests to achieve comprehensive coverage.

Next up: A whole new world awaits. In Chapter 11, we'll delve into the exciting realm of DevOps.

CHAPTER 11

Streamlining Testing with Azure DevOps and Pester

Ready to take your PowerShell scripting to the next level? In this chapter, we'll dive into the world of Azure DevOps, unlocking the power of automated testing and code coverage reporting. We'll explore the magic of YAML (Yet Another Markup Language), crafting a customized script to seamlessly integrate Pester tests into your Azure DevOps pipeline.

Forget tedious manual testing. This chapter empowers you to:

> **Master the Azure DevOps pipeline:** Get hands-on with YAML, understanding its key components without getting bogged down in technical jargon.

> **Unleash Pester's testing prowess:** Configure your pipeline to automatically execute Pester tests, ensuring your scripts are battle-ready.

> **Shine a light on code coverage:** Analyze detailed reports, gaining valuable insights into your code's strengths and weaknesses.

> **Celebrate success with style:** Earn the coveted "Azure Pipelines Succeeded" badge, proudly displaying your testing achievements.

© Owen Heaume 2024
O. Heaume, *Getting Started with Pester 5*, https://doi.org/10.1007/979-8-8688-0306-2_11

So, roll up your sleeves and prepare to unlock a new dimension of efficiency and quality control for your PowerShell scripts. By the end of this chapter, you'll be confidently running automated tests and generating insightful code coverage reports, becoming a true scripting master!

Bridging the Gap: The Purpose of Automation

Having celebrated the prospect of running automated tests and generating insightful code coverage reports, it's crucial to understand the core motivation behind this transition to Azure DevOps.

Why Automate Pester Tests and Code Coverage?

In the dynamic landscape of PowerShell scripting, efficiency and quality control stand as paramount objectives. While manual testing is undoubtedly valuable, the integration of Azure DevOps and Pester aims to elevate your scripting endeavors to new heights. Here's why:

1. **Streamlined Testing Workflow**

   - Automation eliminates the need for manual execution of tests, saving time and effort.

   - Continuous integration (CI) in Azure DevOps ensures that tests run seamlessly with every code change, maintaining a consistent and reliable testing workflow.

2. **Early Detection of Issues**

   - Automated tests, including Pester tests, can swiftly identify potential issues as soon as they arise.

- By integrating testing into the development pipeline,
  you catch bugs and discrepancies early in the process, preventing them from evolving into larger
  problems.

3. **Code Coverage Insights**

   - Code coverage reports go beyond traditional testing
     by providing a visual map of which parts of your
     code are exercised during testing.

   - Insightful reports guide you in strengthening areas
     that may be less tested, enhancing the overall reli-
     ability and resilience of your scripts.

4. **Efficient Quality Control**

   - Automated pipelines ensure that each code change
     undergoes thorough testing, enhancing the overall
     quality control of your scripts.

   - With Azure DevOps integration, you establish a
     standardized and efficient approach to maintain
     high-quality PowerShell scripts.

5. **Continuous Improvement**

   - Regular automated testing and code coverage
     analysis pave the way for continuous improvement.

   - You can iteratively enhance your scripts based on
     feedback from automated tests, fostering a culture of
     constant refinement.

Unlocking a New Dimension

By automating Pester tests and code coverage within Azure DevOps, you unlock a new dimension of scripting efficiency. It's not just about running tests; it's a strategic move toward establishing a robust and streamlined testing process. As you embark on the journey into Azure DevOps in the upcoming sections, envision this integration as a gateway to a scripting realm where efficiency, reliability, and continuous improvement are the guiding principles.

Diving into Azure DevOps – Setting Up the Stage

Let us transform your script testing with the magic of Azure DevOps! The whole of this chapter will take place within the DevOps portal. While setting up a complete DevOps environment falls outside this book's scope, we'll assume you have one ready to unleash its power.

Ready, Set, Code

If you want to follow along, this chapter uses the following files from Chapter 10:

- **Functions.ps1** (Listing 10-1)

- **Functions.tests.ps1** (Listing 10-7)

- **Test.ps1** (Listing 10-8)

Let's begin by integrating these files into your Azure DevOps adventure:

1. **Head to your Azure DevOps project:** Navigate
    to your existing project where you'll house your
    DevOps magic.

2. **Explore the Repo:** Within your project, locate the
    Repos section and select the repository you'll use, in
    this case, named "Demo."

3. **Create a chapter folder:** Inside the repository,
    create a new folder named "Chapter11" to organize
    your files neatly.

4. **Create a src folder:** Inside the Chapter 11 folder
    create a new folder named "src" that will hold our
    functions and tests files.

5. **Upload your files:** Drag and drop your **Functions.ps1**
    and **Functions.tests.ps1** into the newly created
    "**Chapter11\src**" folder and drop **Test.ps1** into the
    Chapter 11 folder as shown in Figure 11-1.

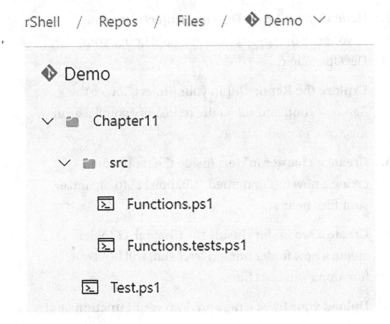

Figure 11-1. *The directory and file structure in DevOps*

By completing these steps, you've successfully planted the seeds for automation within your Azure DevOps project. The next chapter section will guide you through building the YAML pipeline that unleashes the testing power of Pester!

You Ain't My Language, but You're Useful: Working with YAML Pipelines

YAML (Yet Another Markup Language) often gets a reputation for being tricky to grasp. But hey, remember that classic advice, "If you find something difficult, do more of it"? Well, consider this chapter your chance to conquer YAML and unlock its power!

Don't worry; we won't throw you into the deep end. While we won't delve into every intricate detail of YAML, we'll provide a clear and guided walkthrough of the specific YAML file we'll be using. By following along step-by-step, you'll gain practical experience and build confidence in configuring your own pipelines.

So, let's shed the hesitation, embrace the YAML journey, and pave the way for automated testing awesomeness!

Diving into the YAML Depths: Azure-Pipeline.yaml

Alright, deep breath, everyone! Now that we've planted the seeds of automation, let's delve into the heart of our pipeline: the **Azure-Pipeline. yaml** file. Don't let the code in Listing 11-1 scare you! We'll dissect it layer by layer, transforming it into a familiar friend.

Listing 11-1. Azure-Pipeline.yaml

```
trigger:
- main

pool:
  vmImage: windows-latest

steps:
- task: PowerShell@2
  inputs:
    targetType: 'inline'
    script: |
      # Set the working directory
      Set-Location -Path↪ "$(System.DefaultWorkingDirectory)/
      Chapter11"
```

```
    # Run the Test.ps1 script
    .\Test.ps1
  displayName: 'Run Pester Tests'

- task: PublishCodeCoverageResults@1
  inputs:
    codeCoverageTool: 'JaCoCo'
    summaryFileLocation: '$(System.DefaultWorkingDirectory)/
    Chapter11/coverage.xml'⤵
    pathToSources: '$(System.DefaultWorkingDirectory)/
    Chapter11'
  displayName: 'Publish Code Coverage Results'
```

Let's Break It Down

- **Trigger:** This section tells Azure DevOps when to kick off the pipeline. Here, it starts whenever changes are pushed to the "main" branch.

- **Pool:** This specifies the environment where the pipeline runs. We're using a preconfigured "windows-latest" virtual machine.

- **Steps:** This is where the magic happens! Here are the two critical steps:

- **Run Pester Tests**

  - **targetType: 'inline'**: We're defining the PowerShell code directly within the script tag.

  - **Set-Location**: Navigates to the "Chapter11" folder where our files reside.

- **.\Test.ps1**: Executes the `Test.ps1` script, initiating our Pester tests.

- **displayName**: Assigns a user-friendly name for clarity. This appears in the Pipeline console view we will see when running the pipeline.

- **Publish Code Coverage Results**

  - **codeCoverageTool: 'JaCoCo'**: Specifies the code coverage tool (we're using JaCoCo in this example as this is the default tool configured in our Pester configuration item).

  - **summaryFileLocation**: Defines where the code coverage report (`coverage.xml`) is stored.

  - **pathToSources**: Indicates the location of our source code files for analysis.

  - **displayName**: Helps us easily identify this step's purpose.

YAML Quirks: Mind the Spaces!

YAML thrives on order, and that includes spaces. A misplaced space can throw your entire pipeline into chaos! Here's how:

Indentation matters: Indentation defines code blocks and nesting, so pay close attention to those spaces (usually 2 or 4 per level). One wrong indent and your pipeline might not even run.

Colon consistency: Colons (":") mark the end of key-value pairs. Ensure they're always present and followed by a space to avoid errors.

String awareness: Strings enclosed in quotes (")
can be tricky. Watch out for extra spaces within the
quotes, as they become part of the string itself.

Remember, **consistency is key**. Stick to a defined indentation style
and double-check your colons and quotes to keep your YAML pipelines
running smoothly.

Beyond the Surface: Exploring YAML's Potential

While we've navigated the core components of this YAML file, remember
that it's just the tip of the iceberg! YAML in Azure DevOps boasts incredible
flexibility:

Trigger variety: Don't limit yourself to main branch
pushes! Explore triggers based on other pipelines
completing, specific schedules (cron jobs), or even
pull requests.

Operating system choices: Dive beyond Windows!
Run your pipelines on Ubuntu, macOS, or
other supported operating systems to suit your
development environment.

Multi-step mastery: Utilize `strategy:matrix:`
to run identical tasks on different configurations,
testing multiple scenarios with ease.

Template magic: Don't reinvent the wheel!
Leverage templates for common tasks, saving time
and effort.

While delving into all these intricacies falls outside this book's scope, consider them an invitation to explore! Numerous resources await to guide you on your YAML mastery journey. So, experiment, expand your knowledge, and unleash the full potential of Azure DevOps pipelines!

Next Steps

Now that you have a basic understanding of the YAML file, we'll explore how to integrate it into Azure DevOps and witness the automated testing magic unfold! Are you ready to dive deeper?

Bringing Your YAML into Azure DevOps

The first step is to place your YAML file within your Azure DevOps repository. You have flexibility in terms of its location – the example in Figure 11-2 demonstrates one possibility, but it's not strictly required. The important thing is to be able to reference it later in your pipeline.

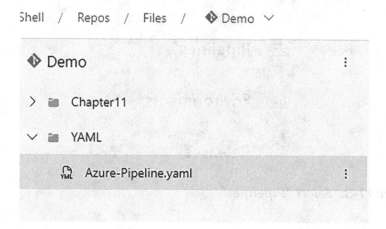

Figure 11-2. *Example placement of Azure-Pipeline.yaml*

Crafting the Pipeline Magic: Bringing Automation to Life

With your YAML file securely nestled in your DevOps repository, let's embark on the exciting journey of creating your Azure DevOps pipeline! This is where the automation magic truly comes alive.

1. **Initiate the Pipeline Wizard**

   - Within your chosen DevOps project, navigate to the **Pipelines** section on the left-hand side menu (Figure 11-3).

   - Click the **New Pipeline** button to kickstart the pipeline creation process (Figure 11-4).

Figure 11-3. Select "Pipelines"

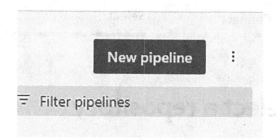

Figure 11-4. *Click "New pipeline"*

2. **Connect Your Code Source**

   – Select the appropriate code repository type. In our
     case, we'll choose *Azure Repos* (Figure 11-5).

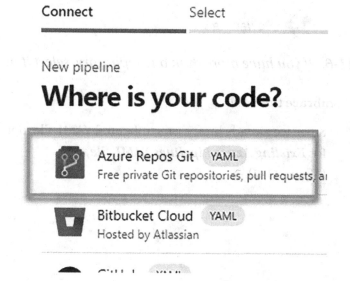

Figure 11-5. *Selecting where our code is stored*

3. **Choose Your Repository**

   – Fromthedisplayedlist,selecttherepositorywhereyourAzure-
     Pipeline.yaml file resides. In this example, we'll pick
     the *Demo* repo (Figure 11-6).

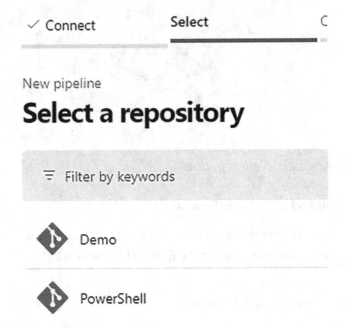

Figure 11-6. *If you have more than one repository, select it here*

4. **Embrace the YAML**

   – Since we already have a preconfigured YAML file, opt
     for *Existing Azure Pipelines YAML file*
     (Figure 11-7).

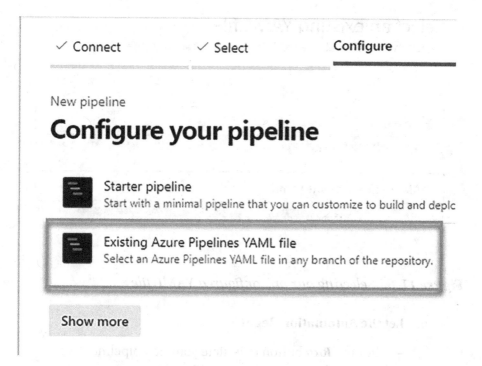

Figure 11-7. *We will select to use our existing YAML file*

5. **Select Your Masterpiece**

    – In the *Path* dropdown menu, locate and select your
      Azure-Pipeline.yaml file (Figure 11-8). Then, click
      Continue.

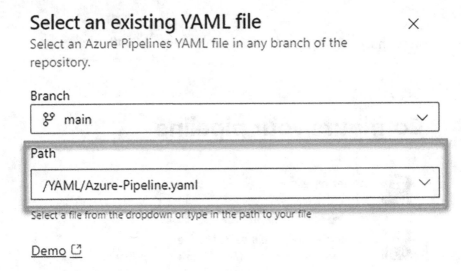

Figure 11-8. *Selecting our preconfigured YAML file*

6. **Let the Automation Begin**

   – Click the **Run** button to initiate your first pipeline execution (Figure 11-9). Watch as automation unfolds!

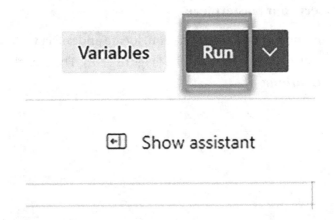

Figure 11-9. *Running the newly configured pipeline*

7. **Pipeline in Action**

   – Head back to the ***Pipelines*** section. Figure 11-10 showcases your newly created pipeline hard at work.

Figure 11-10. The running pipeline!

8. **Dive into the Details**

   – Click the ***Demo*** pipeline to delve into its individual jobs. You'll notice a single job currently, labeled #20240211.1 (Figure 11-11).

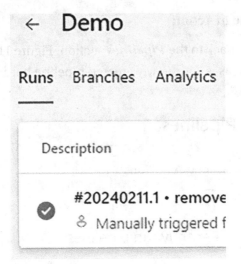

Figure 11-11. *The pipeline jobs*

9. **Unveil the Results**

   – Click the job number to explore its execution details.
     Figure 11-12 shows a successful run (green tick!).
     Click the job itself for an even deeper dive.

Figure 11-12. *Click "Job" to drill into the job just executed and view the results*

10. **Witness Each Stage**

   – Here, you'll see all the pipeline stages laid out. Select
   Pester to view its test and code coverage results, as
   displayed in Figure 11-13.

Here you can view all the stages of your pipeline. If we select "Run
Pester Tests" we can see the results in the console output as shown in
Figure 11-13.

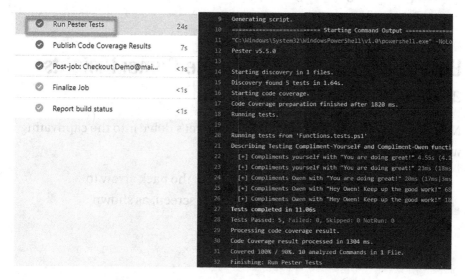

Figure 11-13.   *The pester test and code coverage results*

Congratulations! You've successfully created your first Azure DevOps
pipeline, empowering your Pester tests to run automatically and generate
valuable insights.

Remember   the "main" branch trigger we defined in our YAML file? That means your pipeline has an automation superpower: *automatic execution whenever changes are pushed to the main branch!* So, any code updates or improvements you make will automatically trigger your Pester tests and code coverage analysis, ensuring continuous quality and peace of mind. No more manual testing, just seamless automation doing its magic!

Unraveling the Code Coverage Gems: Insights and Learnings

Now that our pipeline has run successfully, let's delve into the captivating world of code coverage results!

1. **Return to the job summary:** Click the back arrow to navigate back to the job summary screen, as shown in Figure 11-14.

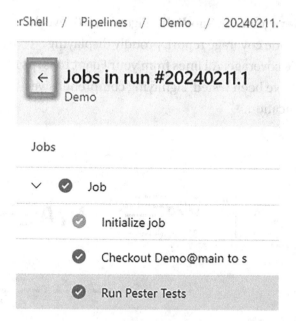

Figure 11-14. *Going back to the previous screen*

2. **Code Coverage awaits:** Look for the ***Code Coverage***
   tab and click it (Figure 11-15). This unlocks the
   treasure trove of insights into your code's coverage.

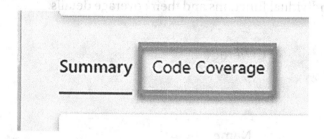

Figure 11-15. *Select the Code Coverage tab*

3. **Coverage in the Spotlight:** Figure 11-16 reveals the code coverage report, proudly displaying 100% coverage! All lines from your `Functions.ps1` file have been tested, signifying comprehensive verification.

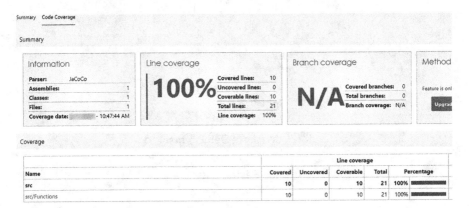

Figure 11-16. *The code coverage report*

4. **Deeper dive:** Let's zoom in for a closer look. Click the **src/Functions** link (Figure 11-17) to examine individual functions and their coverage details.

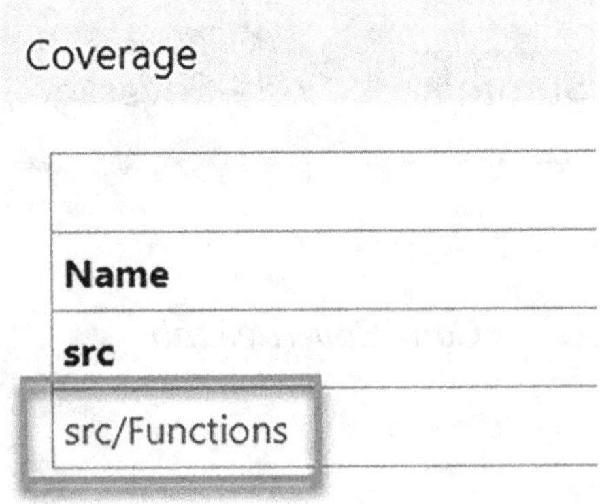

Figure 11-17. *A deep dive into code coverage*

5. **Line-by-line clarity:** Figure 11-18 unveils the granular level of coverage. Each line is highlighted, with covered lines shown in green and uncovered ones (if any) highlighted in red. This precise visualization pinpoints areas needing attention or further testing.

Summary   Code Coverage

Method	Branch coverage	Line coverage
Compliment-Yourself()	-	100%
Compliment-Owen()	-	100%

File(s)

D:\a\1\s\Chapter11\src\Functions.ps1

```
#   Line  Line coverage
    1     function Compliment-Yourself {
1   2         $randomNumber = Get-Random -Minimum 1 -Maximum 3
    3
1   4         if ($randomNumber -eq 1) {
1   5             return 'You are doing great!'
    6         } else {
1   7             return 'Keep up the good work!'
    8     }
```

Figure 11-18. *ViewingCode Coverage function insights*

6. **Simulating failure (for knowledge!):** Remember, learning also involves understanding potential issues. By intentionally removing some tests, I ran the pipeline again. The resulting report (Figure 11-19) displayed individual function coverage percentages (e.g., 75% for Compliment-Yourself) and even highlighted uncovered lines in red (Line 7 in Figure 11-19). This invaluable information helps you identify areas for improvement and ensure comprehensive testing coverage in future iterations.

Metrics

Method	Branch coverage	Line coverage
Compliment-Yourself()	-	75%
Compliment-Owen()	-	83.33%

File(s)

D:\a\1\s\Apress\src\Functions.ps1

#	Line	Line coverage
	1	function Compliment-Yourself {
1	2	$randomNumber = Get-Random -Minimum 1 -Maximum 3
	3	
1	4	if ($randomNumber -eq 1) {
1	5	return 'You are doing great!'
	6	} else {
0	7	return 'Keep up the good work!'

Figure 11-19. *Missed code coverage targets*

As we've explored, the code coverage report offers a wealth of insights into your code's health. By pinpointing uncovered areas, it guides you toward targeted improvements and enhances overall code quality. Remember, strive for high coverage, but also analyze the results critically to prioritize testing efforts effectively.

Now, let's shift gears and explore another exciting aspect of Azure DevOps pipelines: **badges!** In the next section, we'll unveil the "Pipelines Succeeded" badge and learn how to integrate it into your pipeline, providing visual acknowledgment of your testing success.

Earning Your Badge of Honor: Showcasing Pipeline Success

We've established a robust pipeline that executes Pester tests and analyzes code coverage. Now, let's elevate your automation journey with a visible reward: the **Pipelines Succeeded** badge! This coveted badge serves as a visual testament to your successful testing runs, motivating you and fostering a culture of continuous improvement within your team. In this section, we'll unveil the secret sauce for integrating this badge into your pipeline, transforming it into a symbol of pride and achievement. Get ready to display your dedication to automated testing and bask in the glow of well-deserved recognition!

Documenting Your DevOps Prowess: README. md and the Status Badge

Let's add some professionalism and transparency to your project by creating a **README.md** file in your Chapter 11 folder. This file serves as a central hub for anyone exploring the directory, providing context and usage instructions. Figure 11-20 showcases the creation of this file.

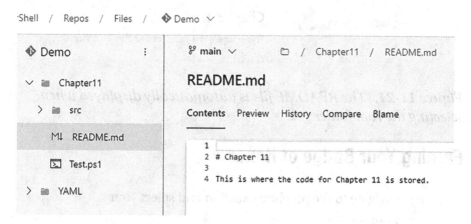

Figure 11-20. *The README.md file*

Once created, selecting the root folder automatically displays the README, as shown in Figure 11-21. Now, let's celebrate your successful pipeline with a visual reward: the "Pipelines Succeeded" badge!

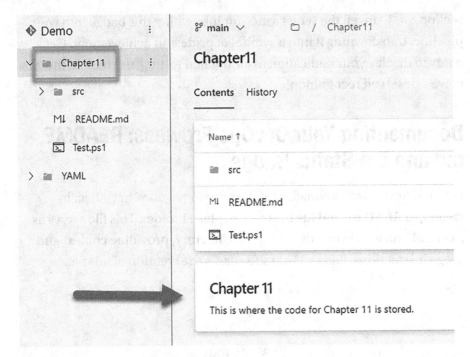

Figure 11-21. *The README file is automatically displayed when selecting the root folder*

Earning Your Badge of Honor

1. Navigate to the pipeline's section and select your pipeline.

2. Click the three dots in the top right corner and
   choose "Status badge" (Figure 11-22).

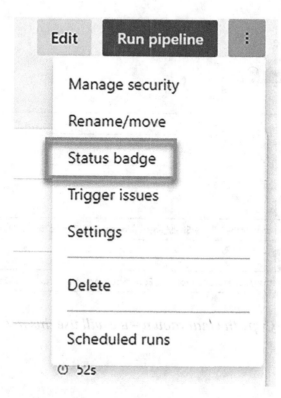

Figure 11-22. *Click the three dots to reveal the menu*

3. Under "Sample markdown," click "Copy" to grab the
   provided code (Figure 11-23).

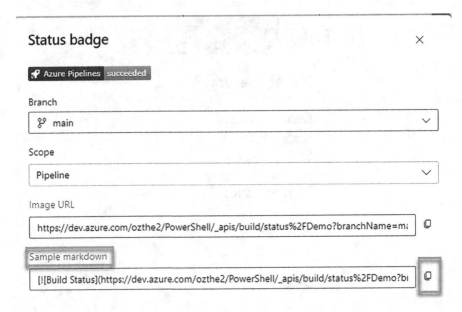

Figure 11-23. *Copy the markdown – we will use this in a moment*

4. Return to your README.md and paste the copied
   markdown near the top (Figure 11-24).

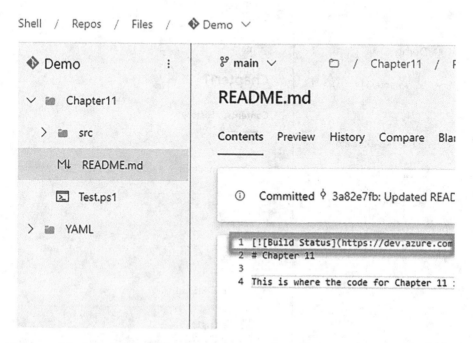

Figure 11-24. Adding the markdown

Voilà! Selecting the root folder now proudly displays your badge of honor, as seen in Figure 11-25.

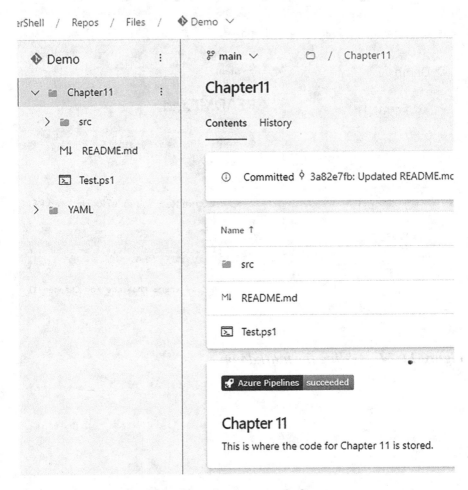

Figure 11-25. *Azure Pipelines has succeeded!*

Testing the Badge's Responsiveness

To demonstrate its dynamic nature, I intentionally introduced Pester test failures. As expected, the badge automatically updated to a "Failure" state (Figure 11-26). Remember, a browser refresh might be needed if the update isn't immediate.

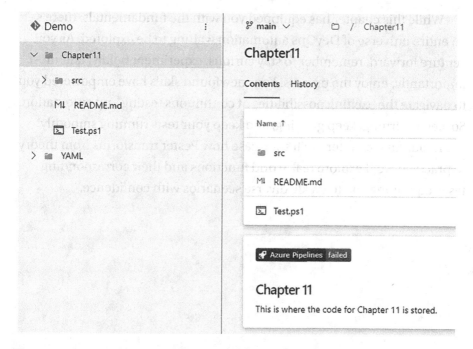

Figure 11-26. *The pipeline has failed*

By incorporating a README and utilizing the status badge, you've added clear documentation and instilled a sense of accomplishment within your DevOps project.

Summary

Congratulations! You've embarked on an empowering journey of automated testing and emerged victorious. This chapter has transformed you from a YAML novice to a masterfully wielding coder, crafting your own Azure DevOps pipeline with confidence.

From triggering Pester tests automatically, deciphering code coverage metrics, and displaying your badge of honor, you've gained invaluable skills that unlock efficiency and valuable project insights. Remember, this is just the springboard of your automation adventure!

While this chapter has equipped you with the fundamentals, there's an entire universe of DevOps automation waiting to be explored. As you venture forward, remember to stay curious, experiment boldly, and most importantly, enjoy the process! Your newfound skills have empowered you to navigate the exciting possibilities of continuous testing and automation. So, keep learning, keep growing, and keep your tests running smoothly!

In our final chapter, we'll showcase how Pester transforms from theory to practice. We'll explore real-world functions and their corresponding tests, equipping you to tackle diverse scenarios with confidence.

## CHAPTER 12

From Theory to Practice: Applying Pester to Your Projects

Congratulations on reaching the final chapter! Now, it's time to witness the power of Pester in action!

This final chapter serves as a showcase, presenting real-world functions and their corresponding Pester tests. (And we also slip in a new data-driven technique to boot!) Though simplified for readability and understandability, the concepts and testing approaches are applicable to more complex scenarios.

Prepare to see Pester in its natural habitat, tackling everyday scenarios and ensuring code quality. Don't worry; we'll highlight any notable aspects along the way, providing valuable insights and practical takeaways.

© Owen Heaume 2024
O. Heaume, *Getting Started with Pester 5*, https://doi.org/10.1007/979-8-8688-0306-2_12

Example 1: A Simple Function

First up, we'll dive into a seemingly simple function: ConvertTo-Uppercase (Listing 12-1). This function takes a string and, as the name suggests, transforms it into uppercase. But don't underestimate its versatility! We'll witness its behavior with various inputs, from lowercase strings to mixed cases and even those containing symbols. In each scenario, Pester will ensure the expected uppercase output as shown in Listing 12-2, demonstrating the power of automated testing.

Listing 12-1. ConvertTo-Uppercase.ps1

```
Function ConvertTo-Uppercase {
    [CmdletBinding()]
    Param(
        [Parameter(Mandatory = $true, ValueFromPipeline ↵
        = $true)]
        [string]$InputString
    )
    Process {
        $InputString.ToUpper()
    }
}
```

Listing 12-2. ConvertTo-Uppercase.tests.ps1

```
BeforeAll {
    . $PSScriptRoot/ConvertTo-Uppercase.ps1
}

Describe "ConvertTo-Uppercase" {
    Context "When converting a string to uppercase" {
        It "Should convert <Text> to <ExpectedResult>" ↵
        -foreach @(
```

```
        @{ Text = "hello world"; ExpectedResult = ↵
        "HELLO WORLD" }
        @{ Text = "Hello World!!"; ExpectedResult = ↵
        "HELLO WORLD!!" }
        @{ Text = "HELLO WORLD"; ExpectedResult = ↵
        "HELLO WORLD" }
        @{ Text = "HelLo WOrlD"; ExpectedResult = ↵
        "HELLO WORLD" }
    ) {
        $result = ConvertTo-Uppercase -InputString $Text

        $result | Should -Be $expectedResult
    }
  }
}
```

In this testing approach, we used data-driven testing to enable multiple test scenarios with ease.

Example 2: Mocking in Action

Mocking, which we covered back in Chapter 9, is a powerful technique for isolating and testing specific parts of your code. Mocking allows you to simulate external dependencies or functions, ensuring your tests focus on the core logic of your function under test.

Imagine we have two functions:

- **Get-FilePath:** Checks if a given file path exists.

- **Remove-FilesSafely:** Removes a file if it exists, otherwise logs a warning.

Testing Remove-FilesSafely directly involves file interactions, which can be inconvenient and potentially dangerous. We do not want to really delete anything. That's where mocking comes in! (For convenience, all functions and tests are included in Listing 12-3, so it may be run as-is.)

Listing 12-3. The functions and tests all-in-one file for convenience

```
function Get-FilePath {
    [CmdletBinding()]
    Param(
        [Parameter(Mandatory = $true)]
        [string]$FilePath
    )

    Test-Path -Path $FilePath
}

function Remove-FilesSafely {
    [CmdletBinding()]
    Param(
        [Parameter(Mandatory = $true, ValueFromPipeline ↰
        = $true)]
        [string]$FilePath
    )

    if (Get-FilePath $FilePath) {
        Remove-Item -Path $FilePath -Force
    } else {
        Write-Warning "Invalid file path provided: $FilePath"
    }
}

Describe Remove-FilesSafely {
    Context "When removing files safely" {
        It "Should remove the file" {
```

```
        Mock Get-FilePath { $true }
        Mock Remove-Item { }

        Remove-FilesSafely -FilePath "C:\myFolder\file.tmp"

        Should -Invoke Get-FilePath -Exactly -Times 1
        Should -Invoke Remove-Item -Exactly -Times 1
    }
}

Context "If the path is invalid" {
    It "Should not remove the file" {
        Mock Get-FilePath { $false }
        Mock Remove-Item { }
        Mock Write-Warning { }

        Remove-FilesSafely -FilePath↩ "C:\myFolder\
        file.tmp"

        Should -Invoke Get-FilePath -Exactly -Times 1
        Should -Invoke Remove-Item -Exactly -Times 0
        Should -Invoke Write-Warning -Exactly -Times 1
    }
}
}
```

Running this code products the expected output as shown in Figure 12-1.

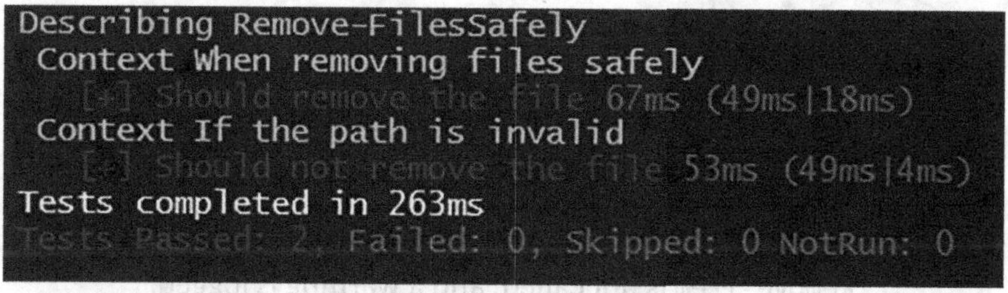

Figure 12-1. The expected test results

Code Breakdown

Here is a brief code breakdown of the tests. If you feel you need more explanation, turn back a few pages to Chapter 9 and refresh your memory!

Functions

- **Get-FilePath:** This simple function uses Test-Path to verify if a file exists.

- **Remove-FilesSafely:** This function checks if the file exists using Get-FilePath and removes it if so. It logs a warning if the file doesn't exist.

Tests

- We use Pester's **Mock** function to simulate both Get-FilePath and Remove-Item (used internally for removal).

- **Valid Path**

  - We mock Get-FilePath to return $true, simulating a valid file path.

  - We verify that Get-FilePath and Remove-Item are called once each.

- **Invalid Path**

  - We mock Get-FilePath to return $false, simulating an invalid path.

  - We verify that Get-FilePath is called once, Remove-Item is not called, and a warning is logged.

Example 3: Unleashing Data Clarity: Data-Driven Testing with a Twist

Data-driven testing is a powerhouse for streamlining test creation, but deciphering complex code with nested loops can be daunting. In this example, we'll leverage a technique that enhances readability and flexibility without compromising efficiency.

Revisiting "ConvertTo-Uppercase"

Remember the ConvertTo-Uppercase function from Example 1? We'll revisit it, but this time, we'll employ a powerful technique for data-driven testing.

Introducing the *Data* Construct (Listing 12-4).

Listing 12-4. Using the Data construct for code clarity and flexibility

```
BeforeAll {
    . $PSScriptRoot/ConvertTo-Uppercase.ps1
}

Describe "ConvertTo-Uppercase" {
    Context "When converting a string to uppercase" {
        data testData {
            @{Text = "hello world";   ExpectedResult = ↩
            "HELLO WORLD" }
            @{Text = "Hello World!!"; ExpectedResult = ↩
            "HELLO WORLD!!" }
            @{Text = "HELLO WORLD";   ExpectedResult = ↩
            "HELLO WORLD" }
            @{Text = "HelLo WOrlD";   ExpectedResult = ↩
            "HELLO WORLD" }
        }
```

```
It "Should convert <Text> to <ExpectedResult>" ↵
-ForEach $testData {
    $result = ConvertTo-Uppercase -InputString $Text

    $result | Should -Be $expectedResult
}
}
}
```

Remember   The magic starts with the **Data** keyword! This defines your data set, but feel free to swap "testData" for any name that suits your fancy. Just keep it consistent when calling it within the `-ForEach` loop. This flexibility allows you to easily reuse the data in other tests within the same context, adding another layer of efficiency and organization to your testing endeavors.

The Outcome

Figure 12-2 displays the expected test results.

```
Describing ConvertTo-Uppercase
  Context When converting a string to uppercase
    [+] Should convert hello world to HELLO WORLD 185ms
    [+] Should convert Hello world!! to HELLO WORLD!! 9
    [+] Should convert HELLO WORLD to HELLO WORLD 4ms (
    [+] Should convert HeLLo World to HELLO WORLD 8ms (
Tests completed in 506ms
Tests Passed: 4, Failed: 0, Skipped: 0 NotRun: 0
```

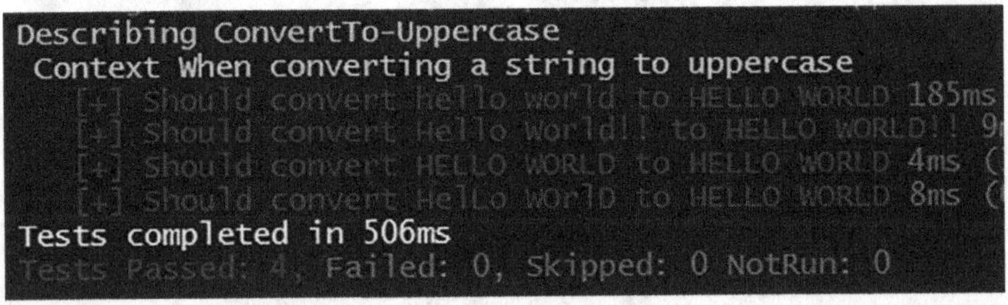

Figure 12-2. *The expected test results*

The Final Analogy

It has been a few chapters now where I have not included an analogy, so let's use one for the final time ...

Imagine your Pester tests as a grand stage play. Each test case is an individual act, carefully crafted to showcase the functionality of your code. But as the number of acts grows, managing the props and remembering everyone's lines can become chaotic.

Enter the **data** construct, your backstage hero! It's like a dedicated prop room, neatly storing all the costumes, scripts, and stage directions for each act. This frees up the actors (your test cases) to focus on delivering their best performances without tripping over props or fumbling with lines.

Here's the magic:

Clarity: Instead of props scattered across the stage, the "data" construct keeps everything organized and easily accessible. Think of it as a well-lit prop room with labeled shelves, making it a breeze for anyone (even understudies!) to find what they need.

Flexibility: Need to add a new scene (test case)? Simply add the props and script to the "data" room. No need to rewrite entire acts – just reference the new props in your existing test cases. It's like having a versatile wardrobe that can adapt to any scene with minimal effort.

Reusability: Remember those fancy costumes from Act 1? They can reappear in Act 3! With the "data" construct, you can reuse data across multiple test cases, saving time and effort while ensuring consistency. Think of it as a costume rental service for your entire play, maximizing resources and avoiding redundancy.

So, the next time you find yourself juggling props and lines in your Pester tests, remember the "data" construct – your backstage hero for clarity, flexibility, and reusability!

Summary

This chapter revealed the true potential of Pester by demonstrating its capabilities in a real-world testing environment. We began with a simple conversion function, ensuring quality as you learned how to organize tests for readability and reuse. Next, you conquered the art of mocking and isolating code sections to guarantee that even functions depending on external interactions can be seamlessly tested. Finally, you discovered how to streamline data-driven testing with the "Data" construct, enhancing clarity and flexibility within your testing practices.

Key Takeaways

Testing is essential: Automated testing with Pester safeguards the quality and correctness of your code, empowering you to make changes confidently.

Readability matters: Well-structured tests, like those using data-driven techniques, increase maintainability and promote easy test updates.

Isolation for precision: Mocking lets you test the core logic of your code without depending on tricky external factors.

Pester in the real world: The examples in this chapter are more than theoretical; the concepts discussed translate directly to your everyday PowerShell development scenarios.

Moving Forward

As you continue your Pester journey, don't be afraid to get creative! Look for opportunities to automate different tests within your own projects, experimenting with the techniques we've explored. Pester will become your invaluable companion, ensuring your PowerShell code functions as intended and allowing you to focus on delivering great results.

Index

Printed in the United States
by Baker & Taylor Publisher Services